Real World
Colouring Book
For Advanced Users & Adults

Copyright 2019 By John Boom

50 Images

Created From Real Life Photos
For You To Colour As You Please.

ISBN 978-0-359-78810-1

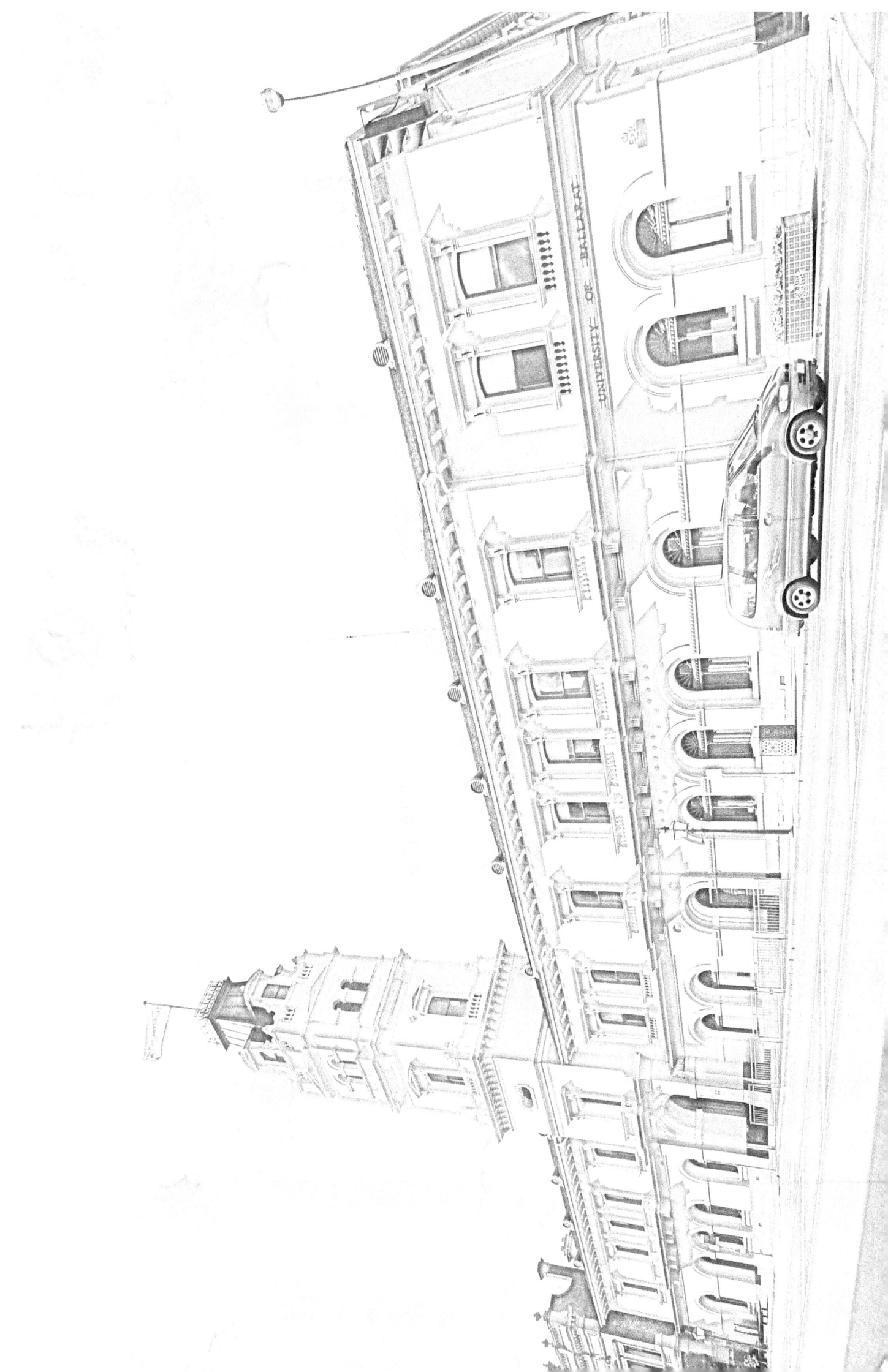

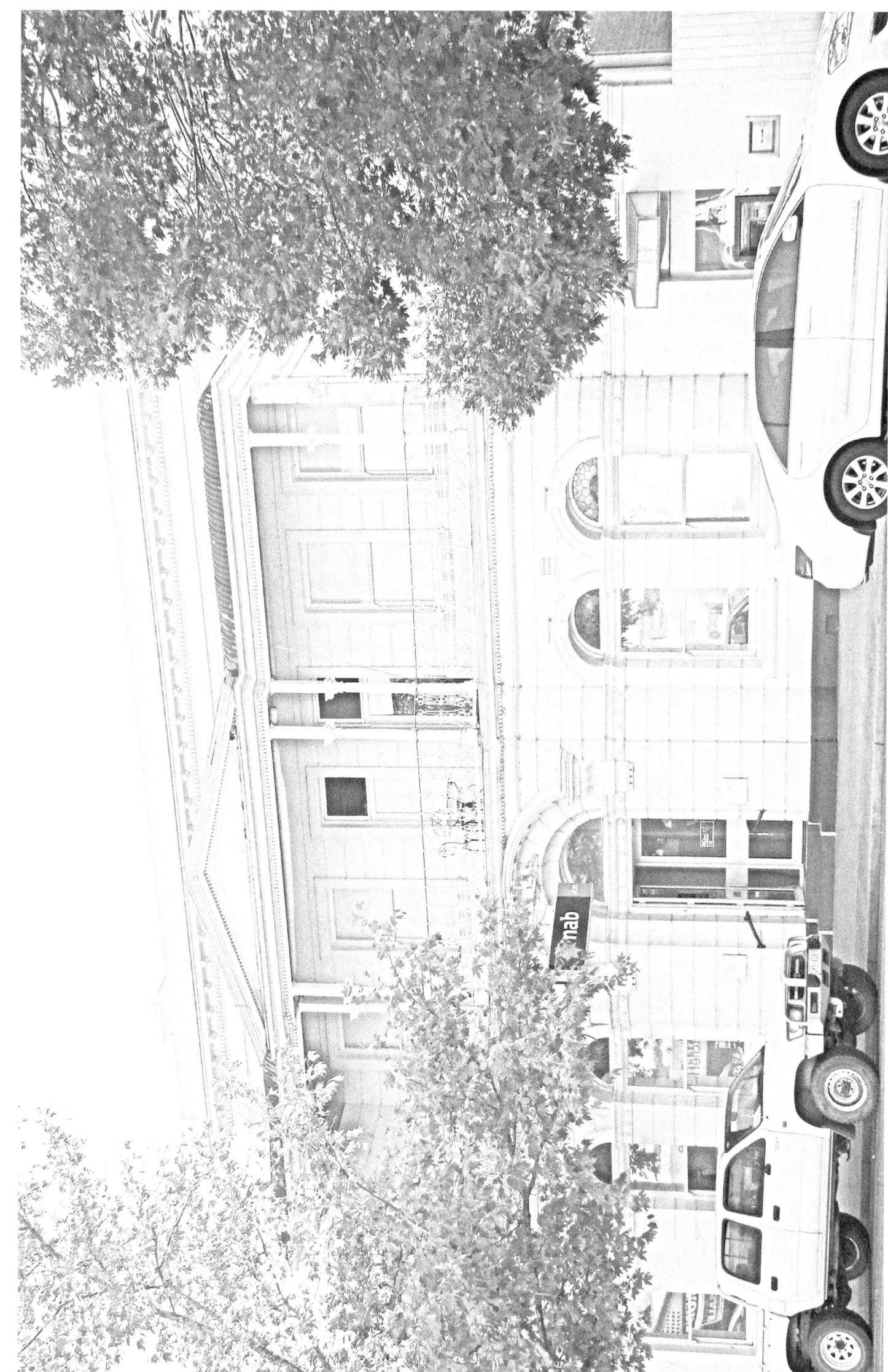

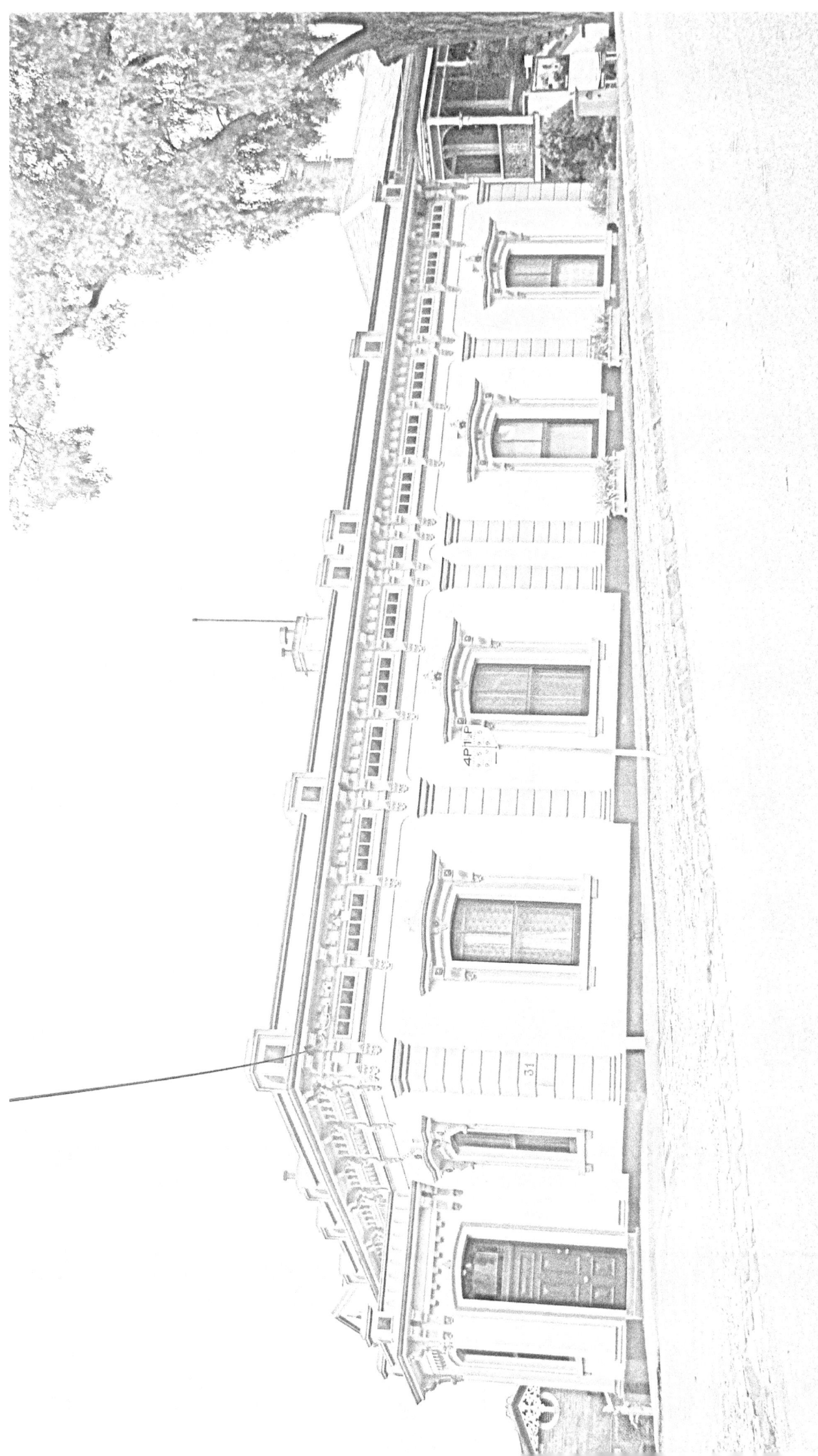

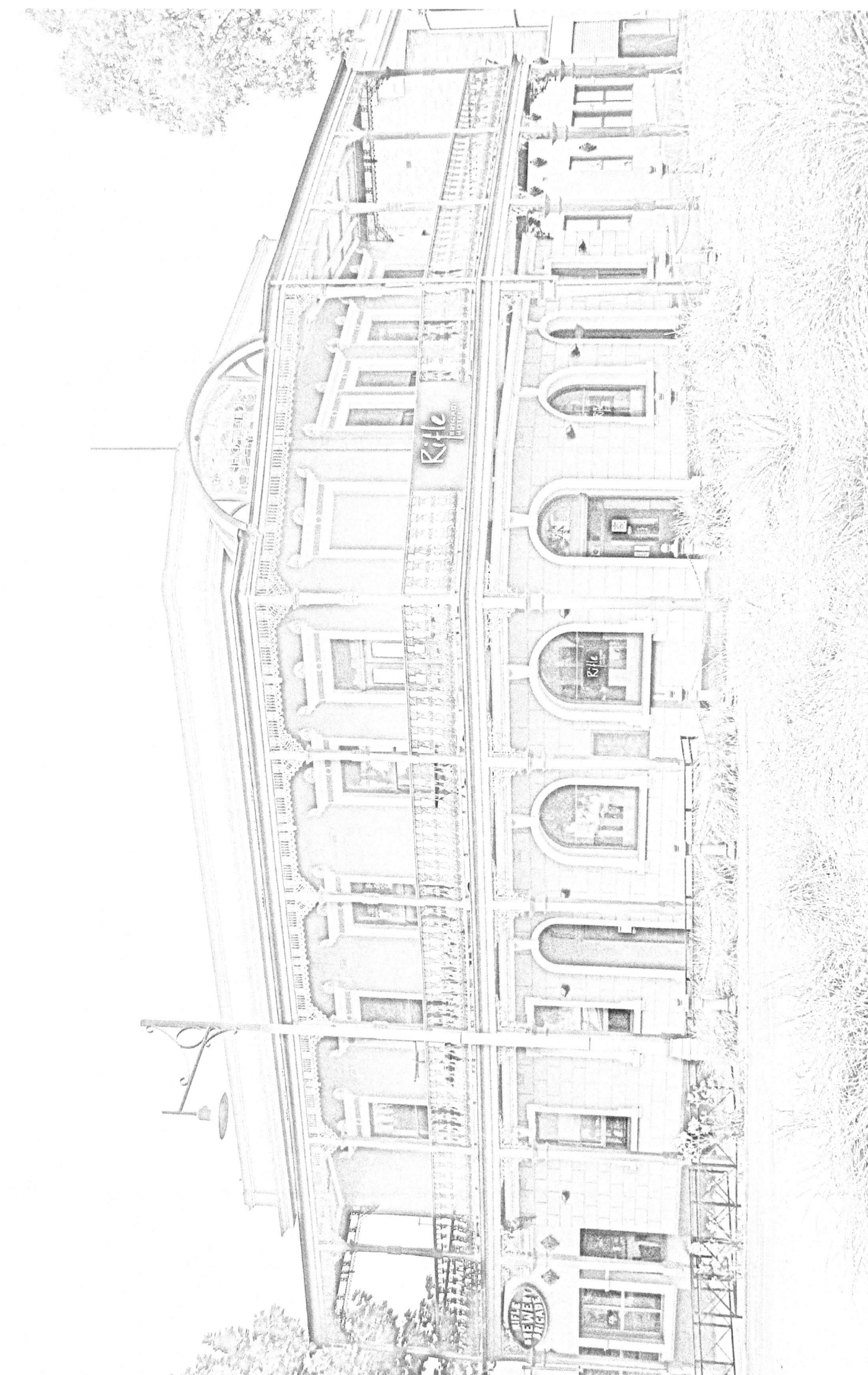

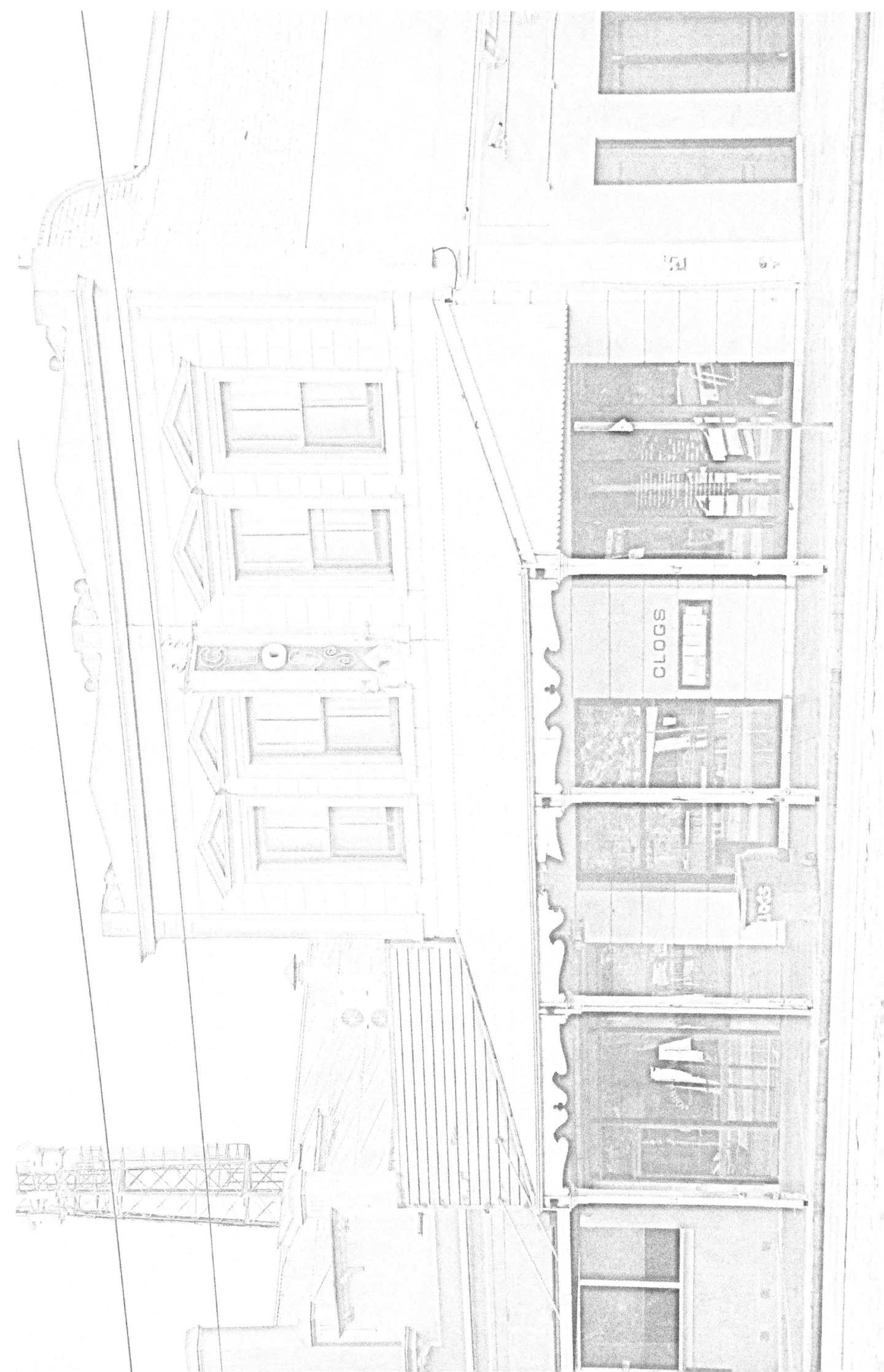

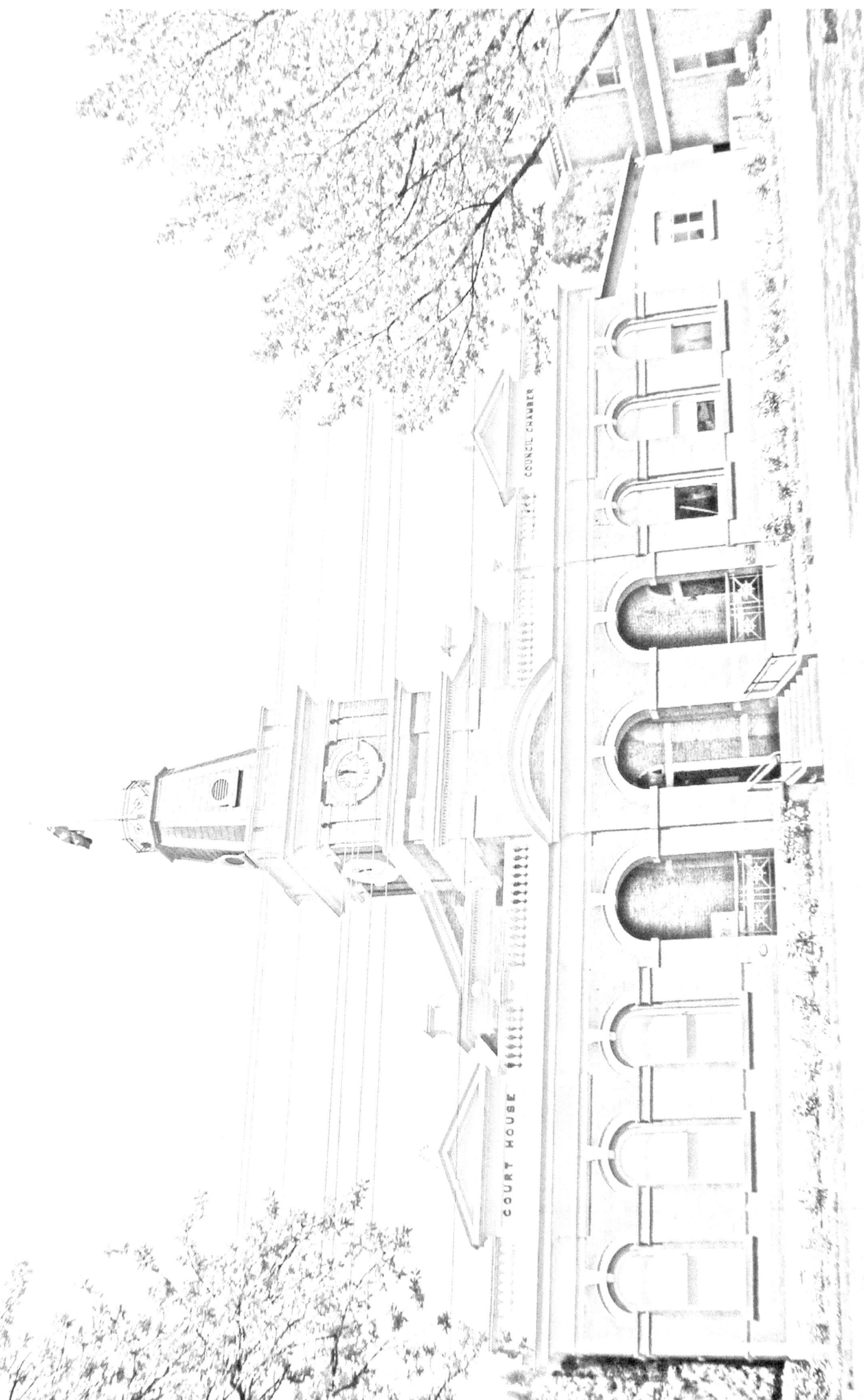

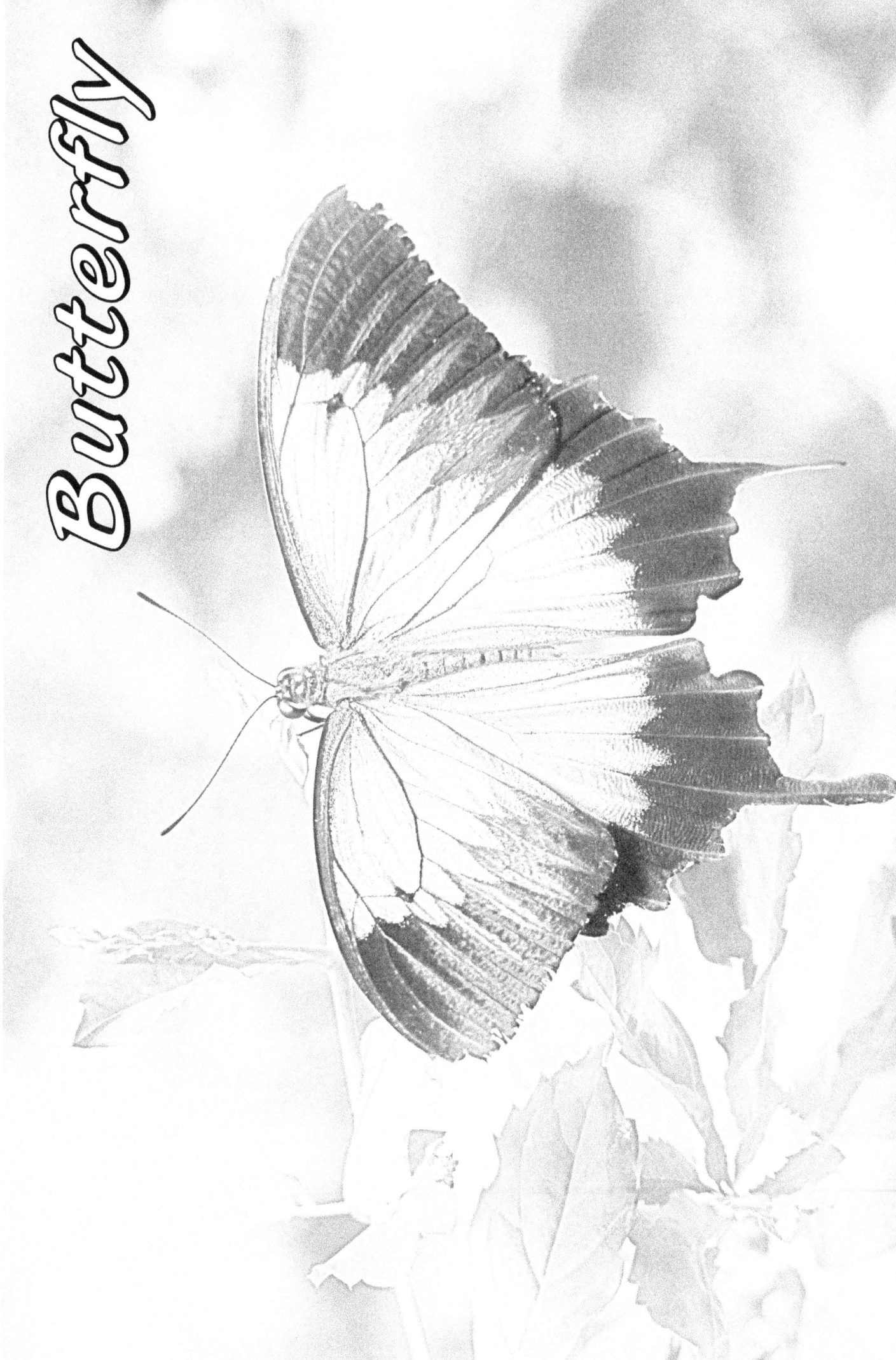

Butterfly

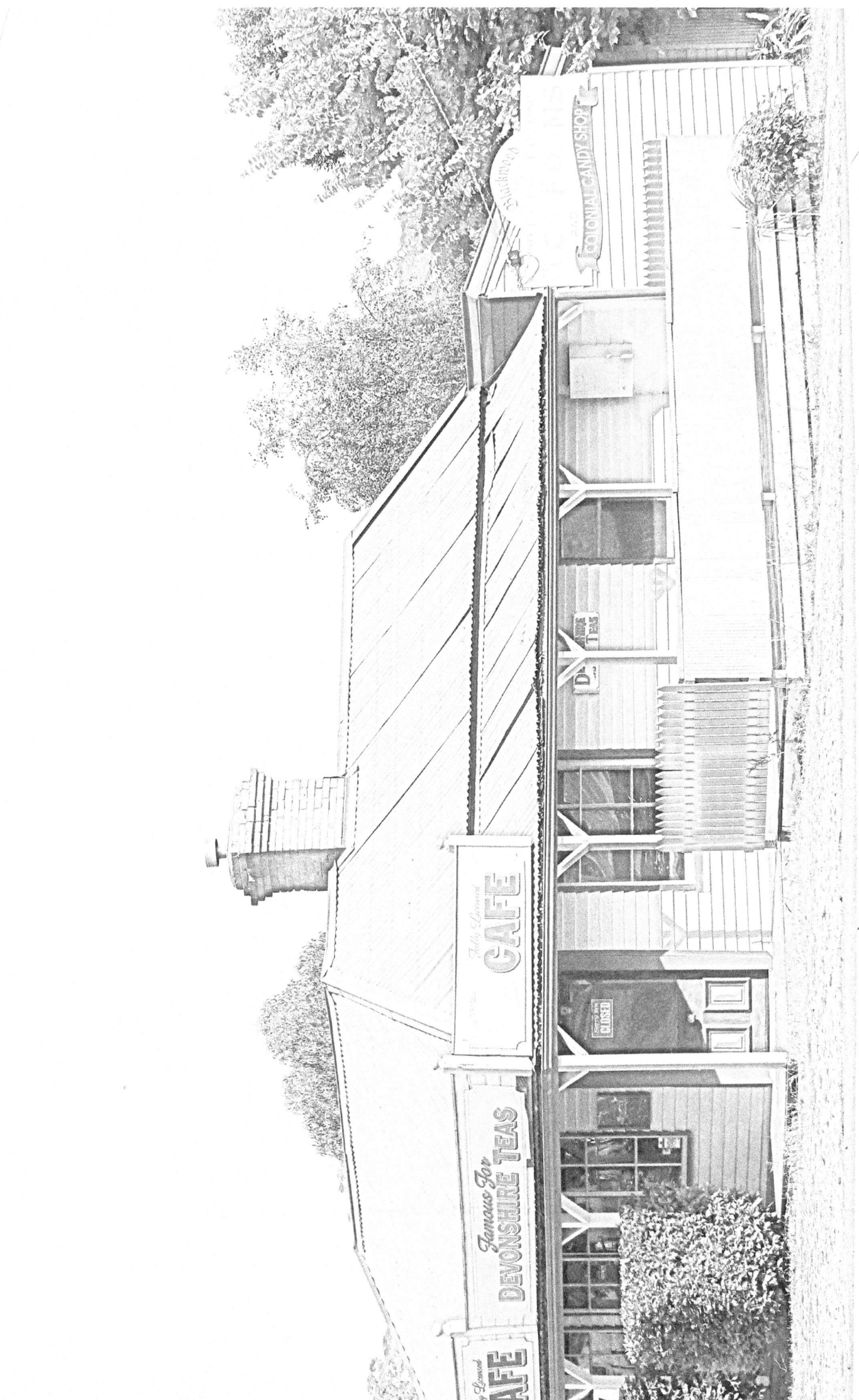

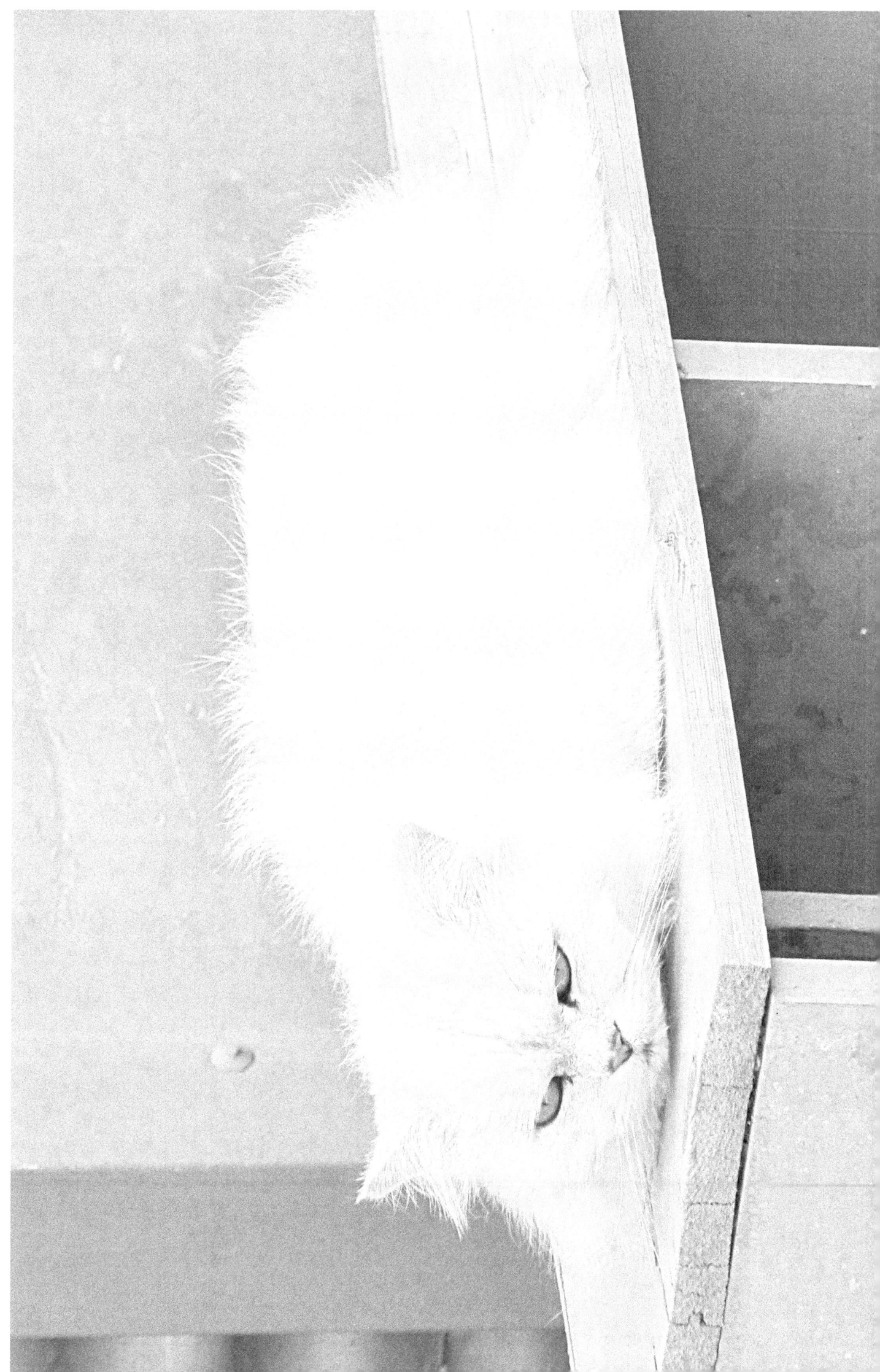

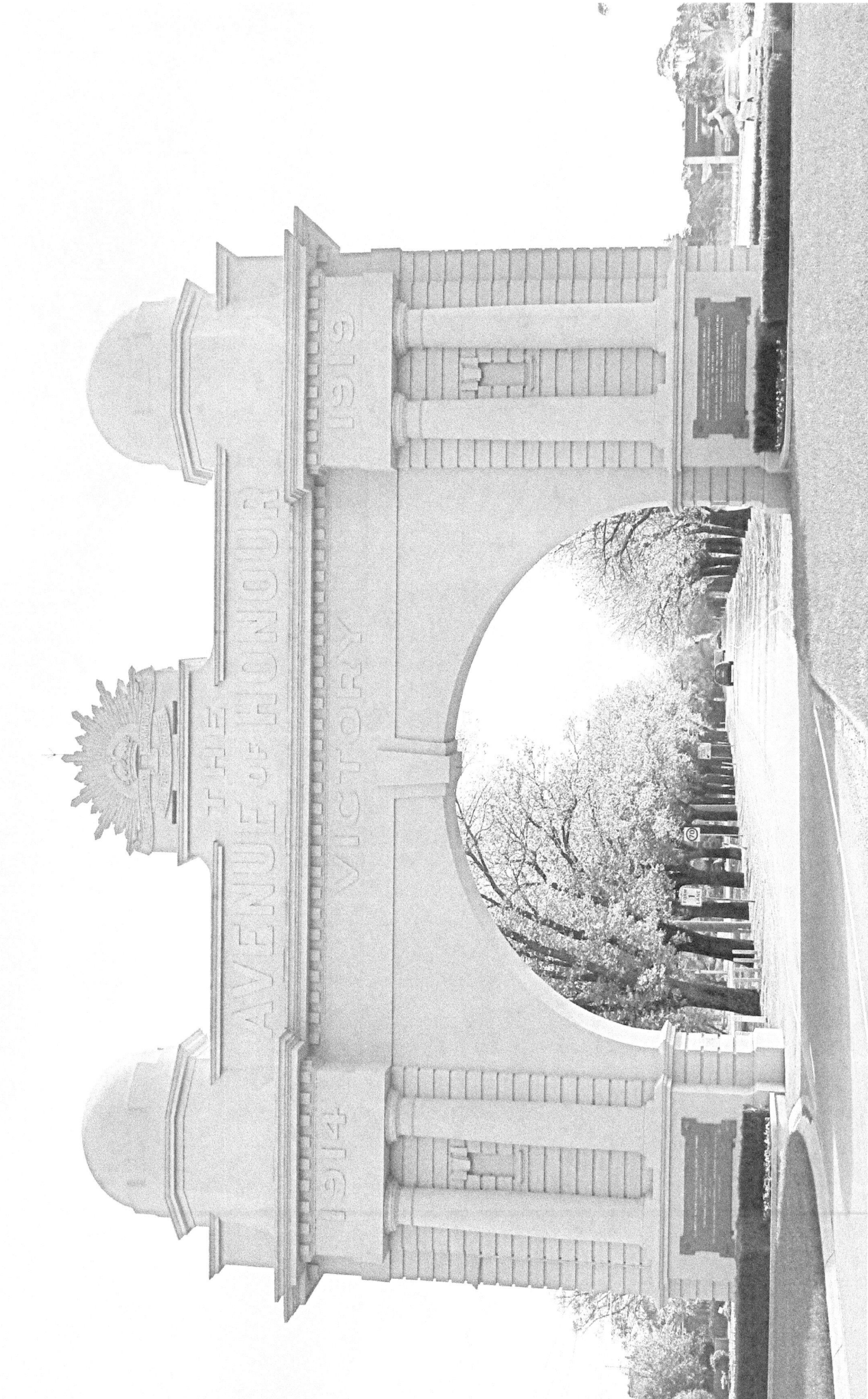

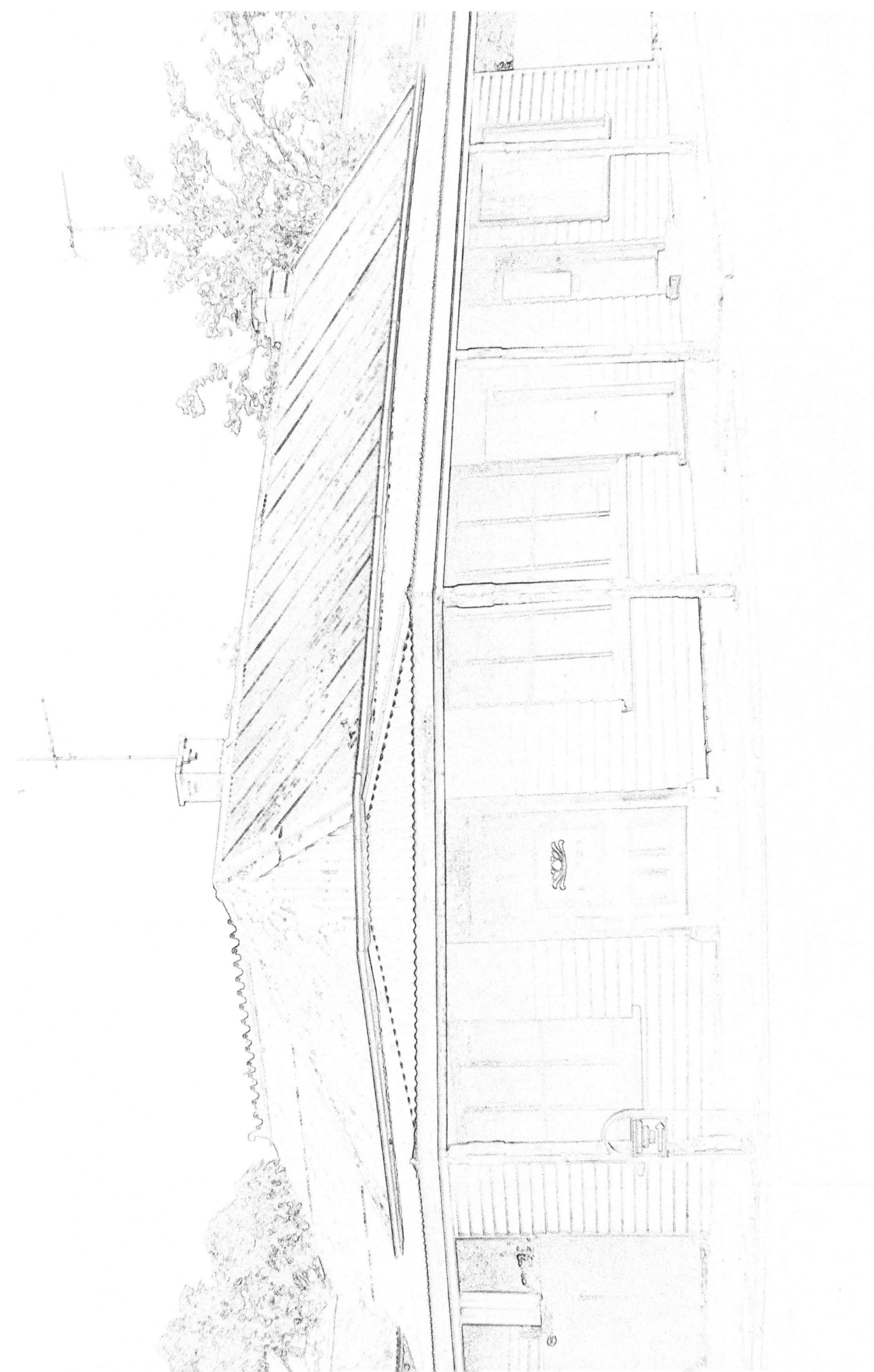

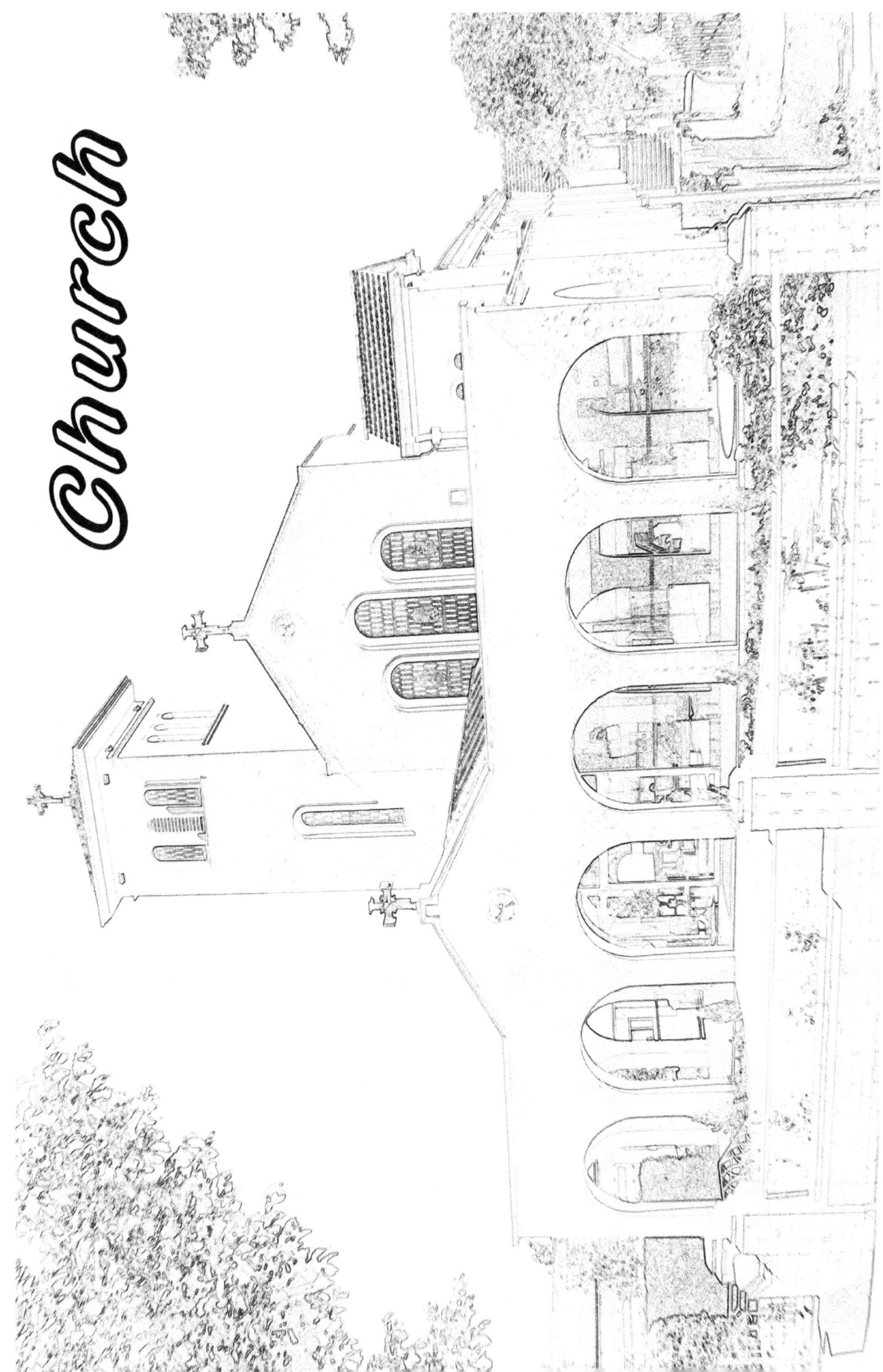

Church

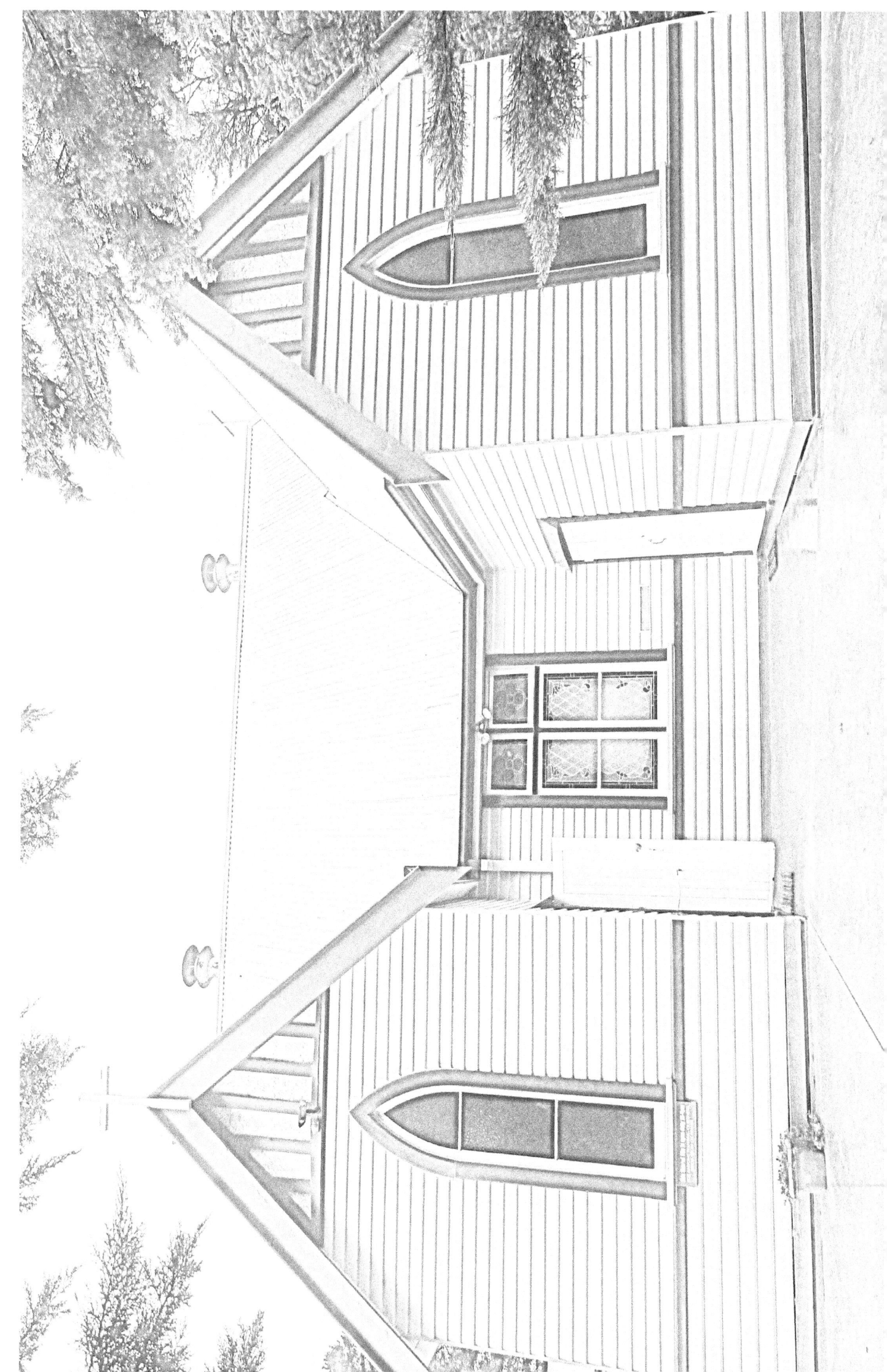

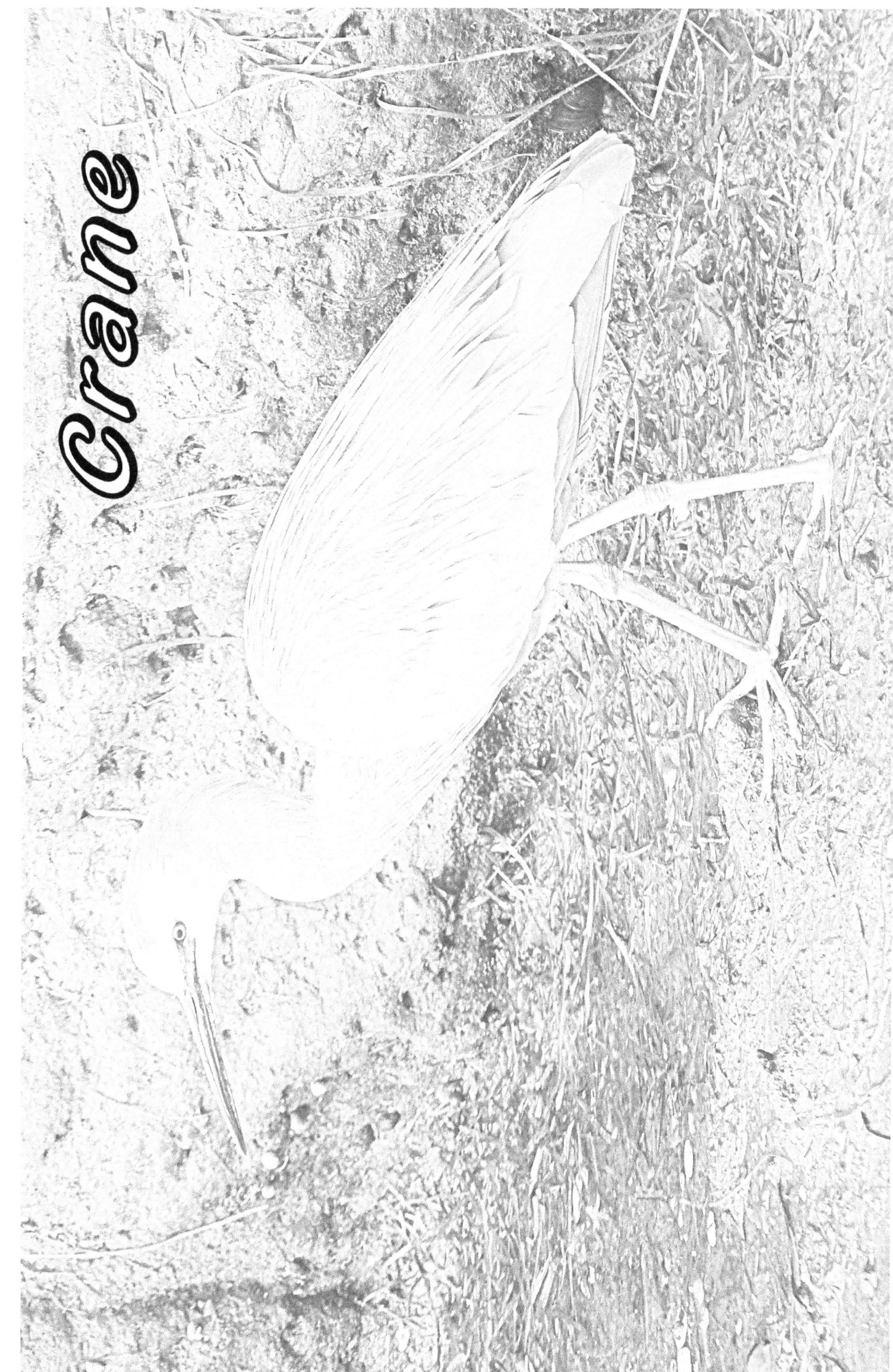

Crane

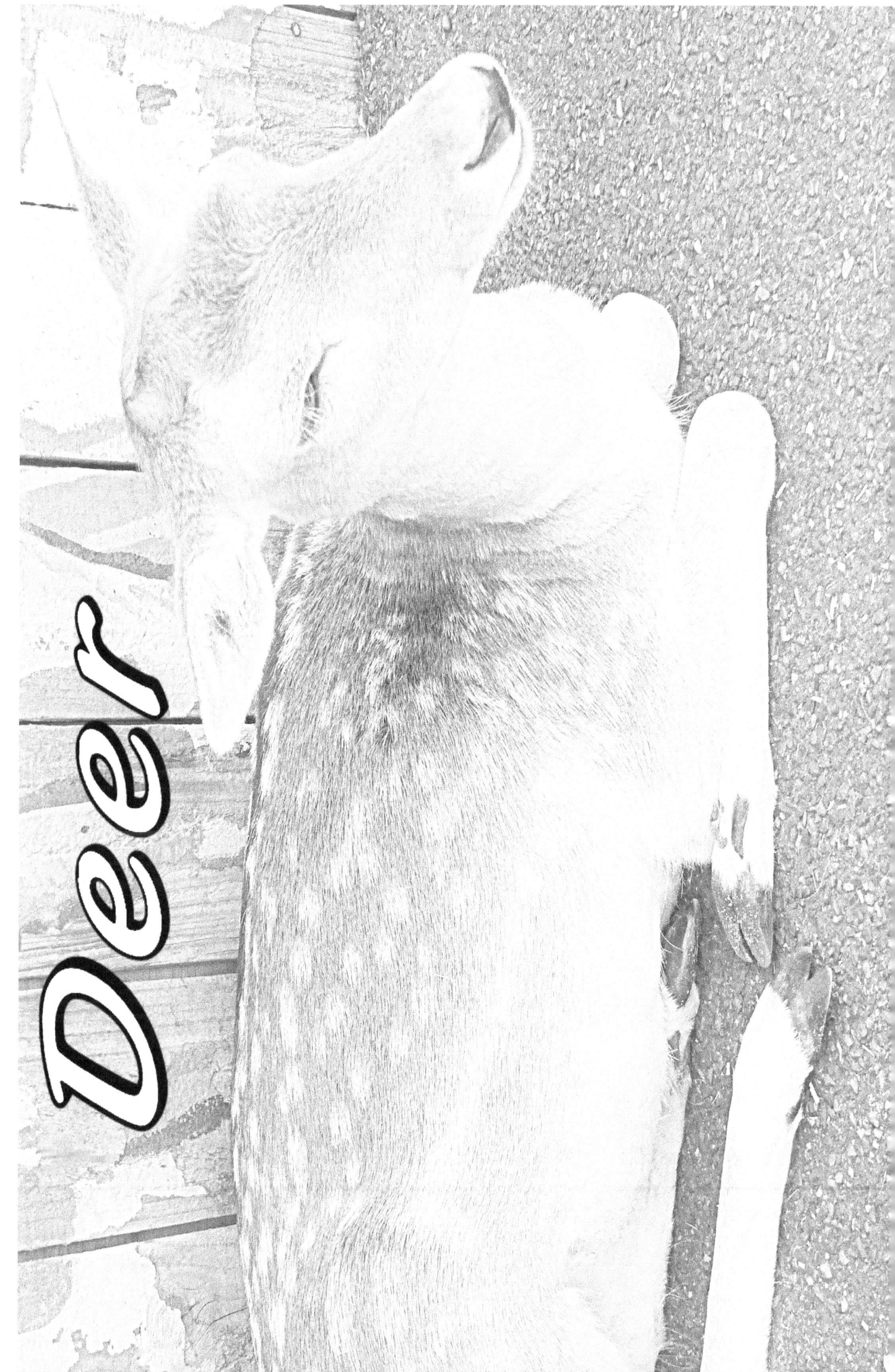

Deer

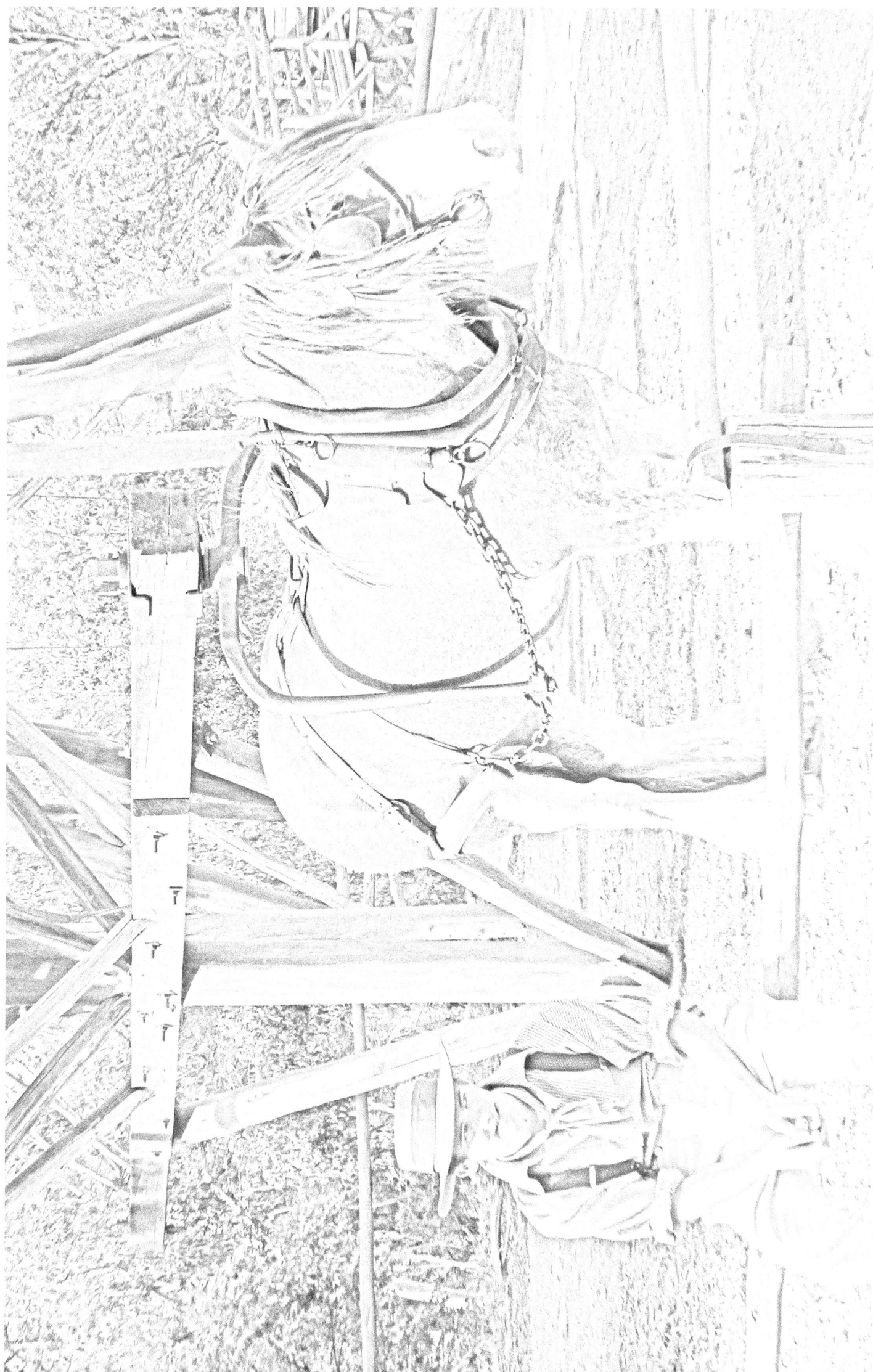

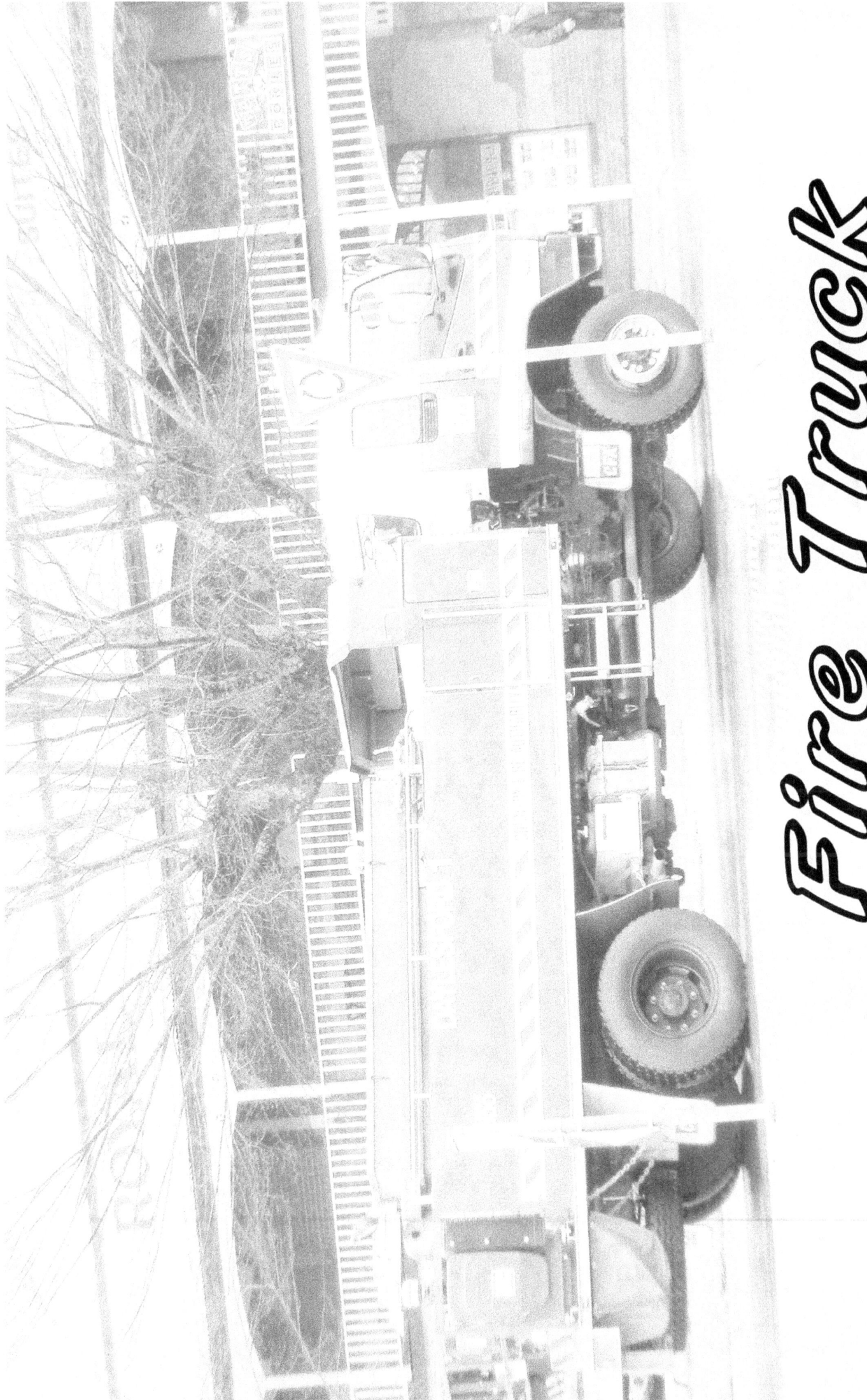

Fire Truck

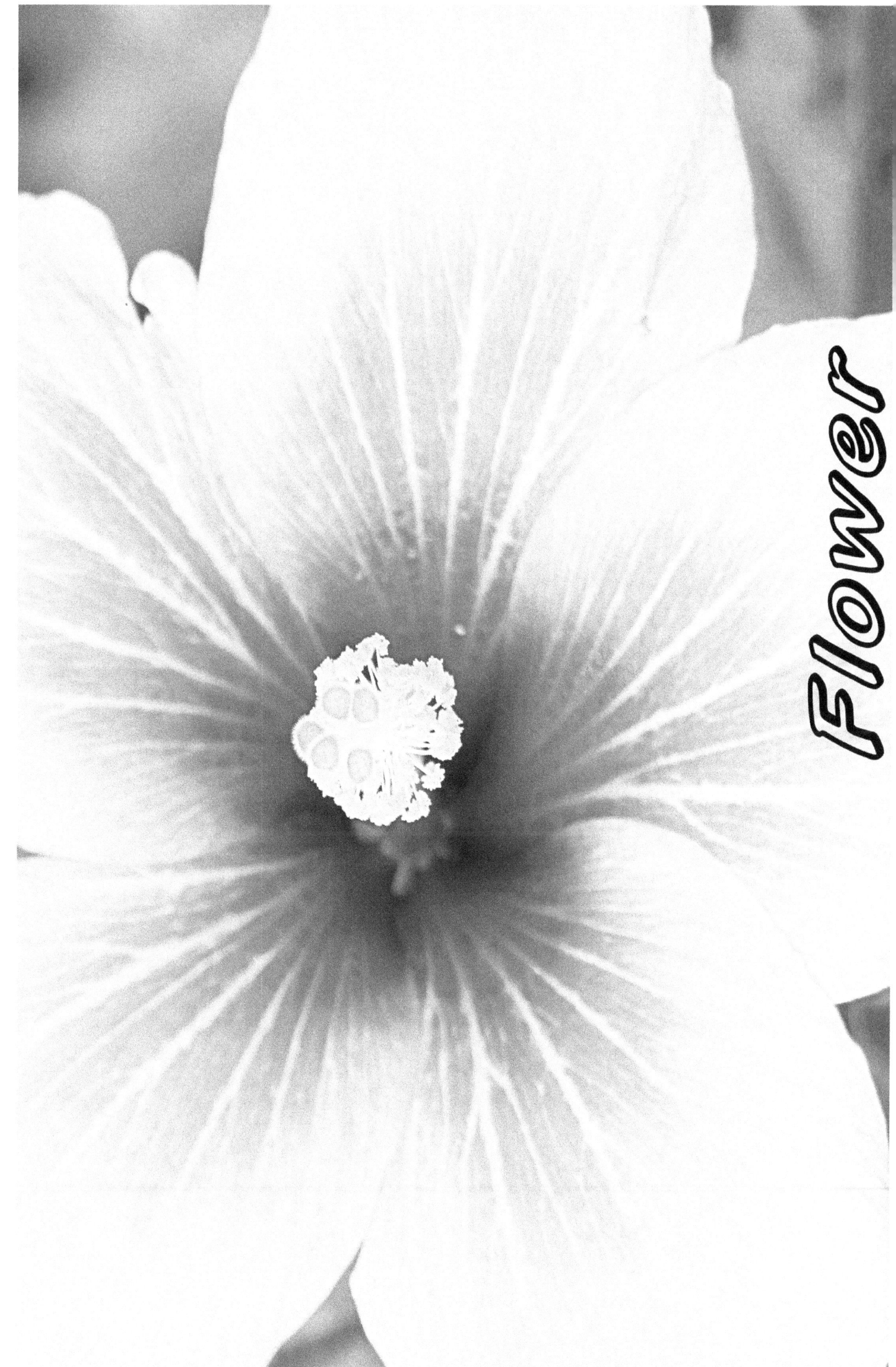

Flower

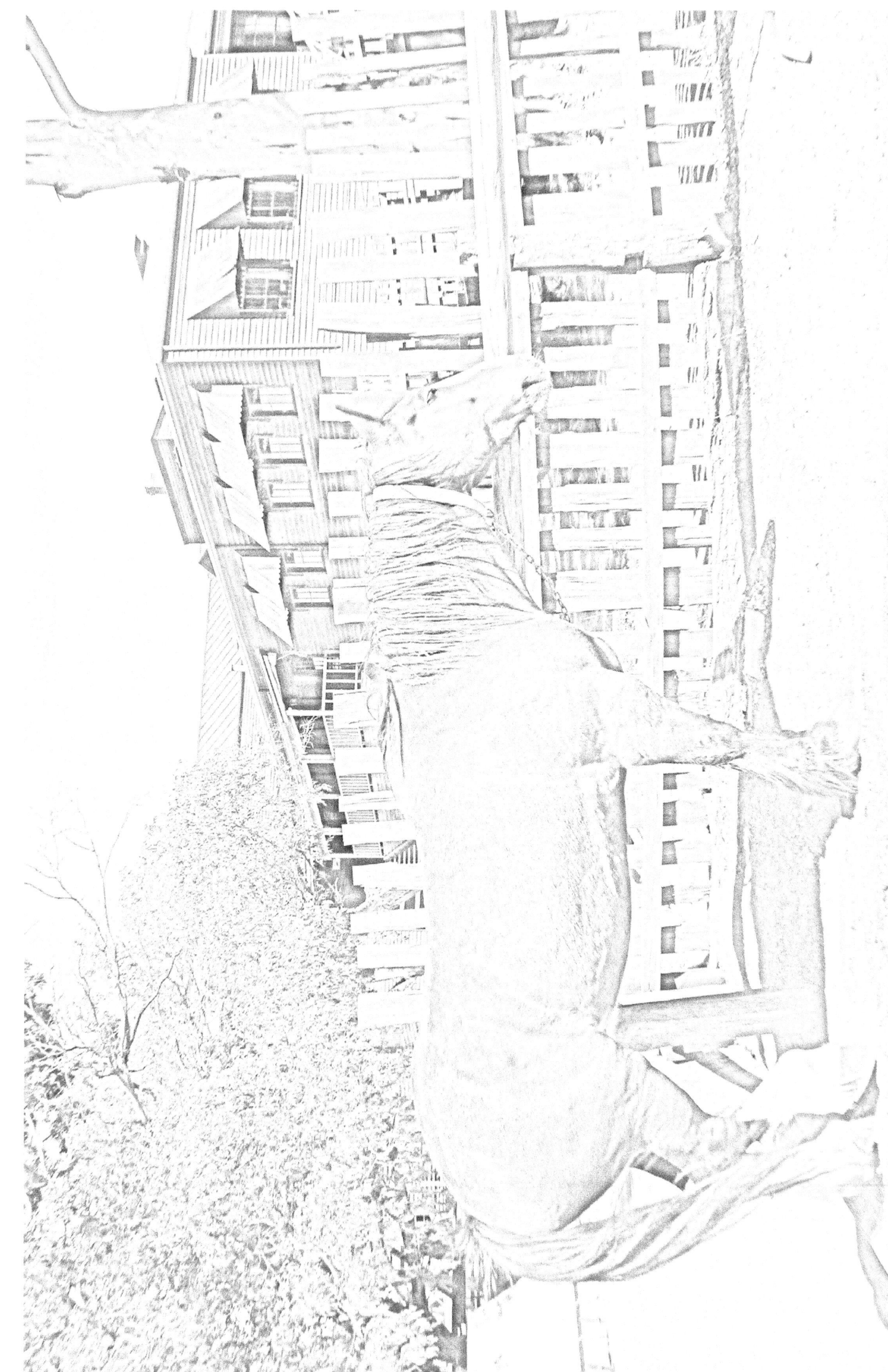

Hotel

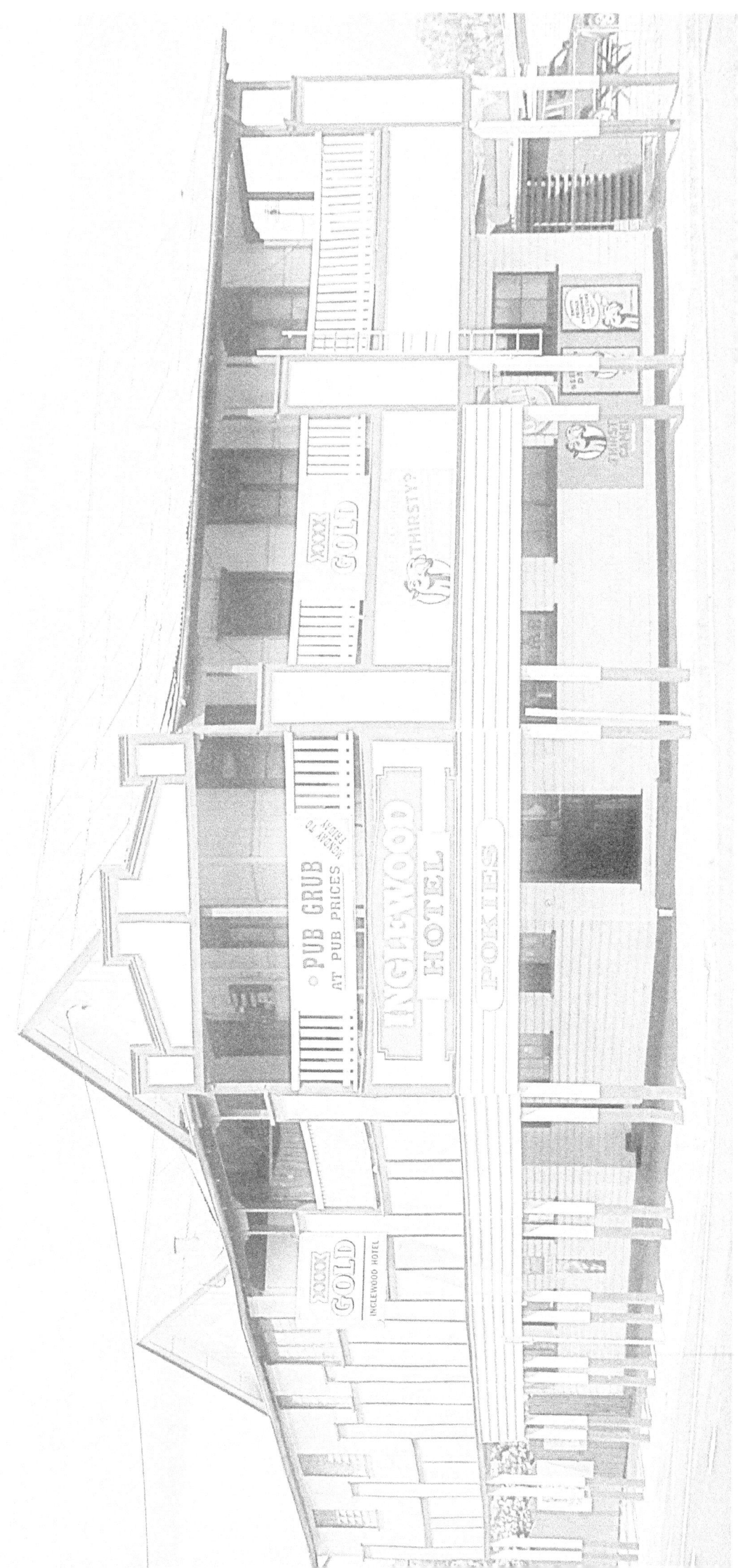

Hotel

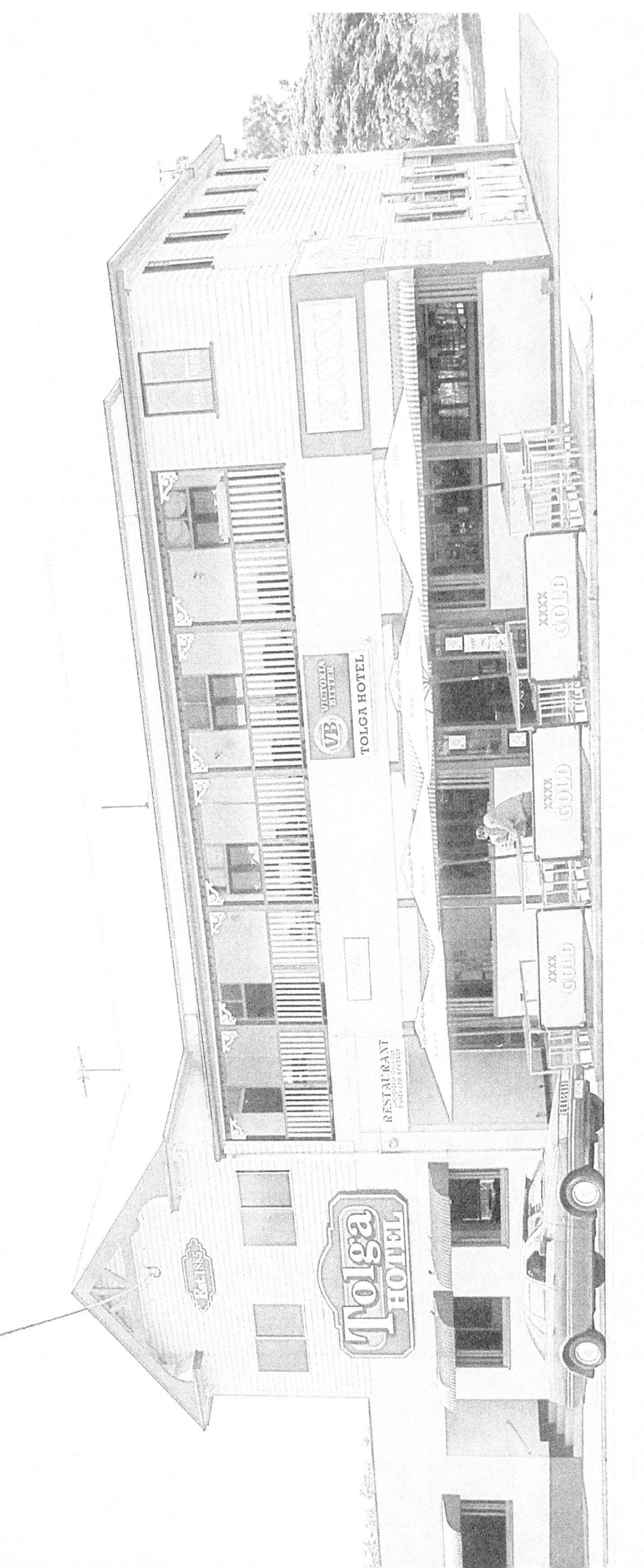

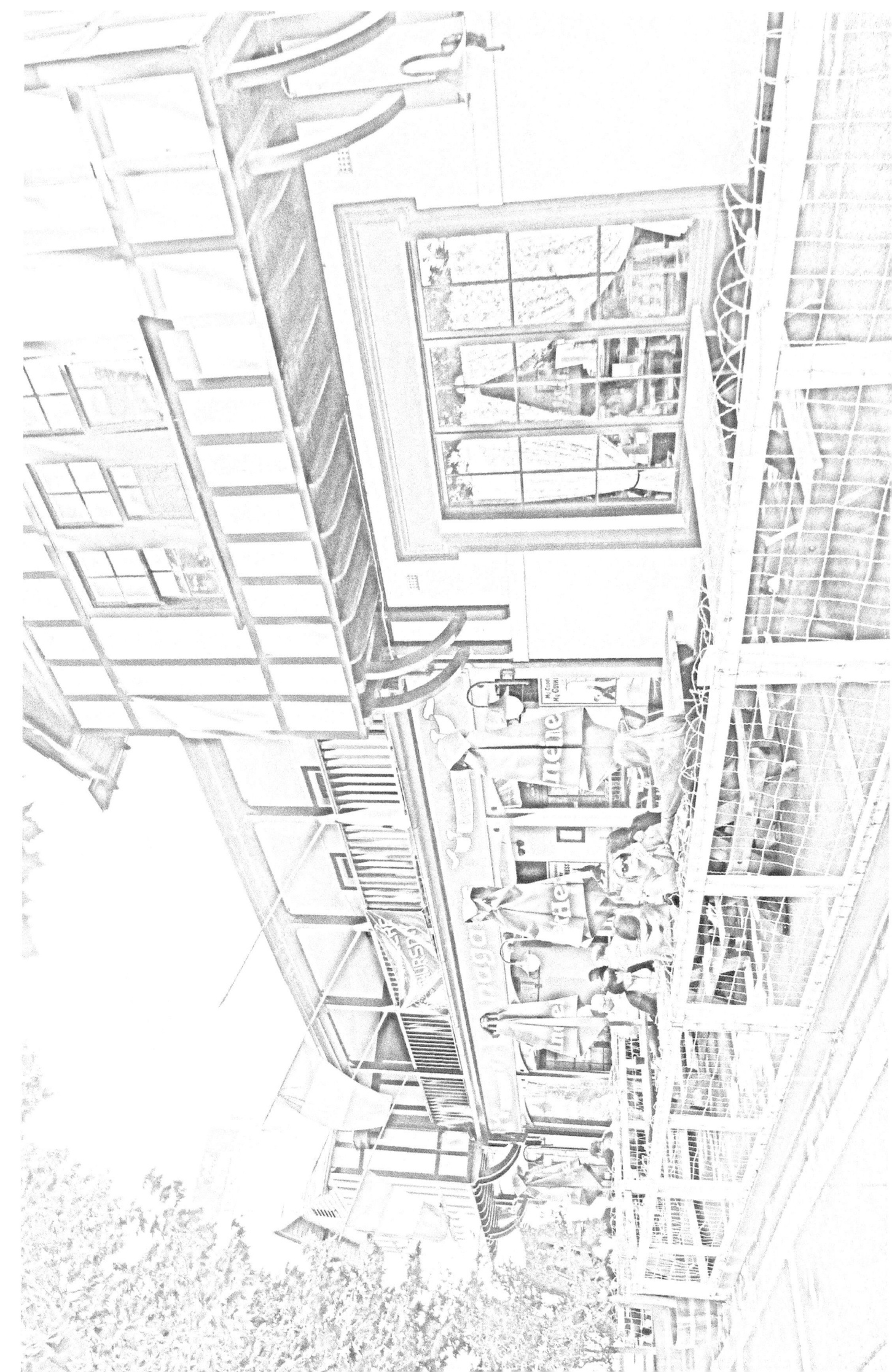

Hotel

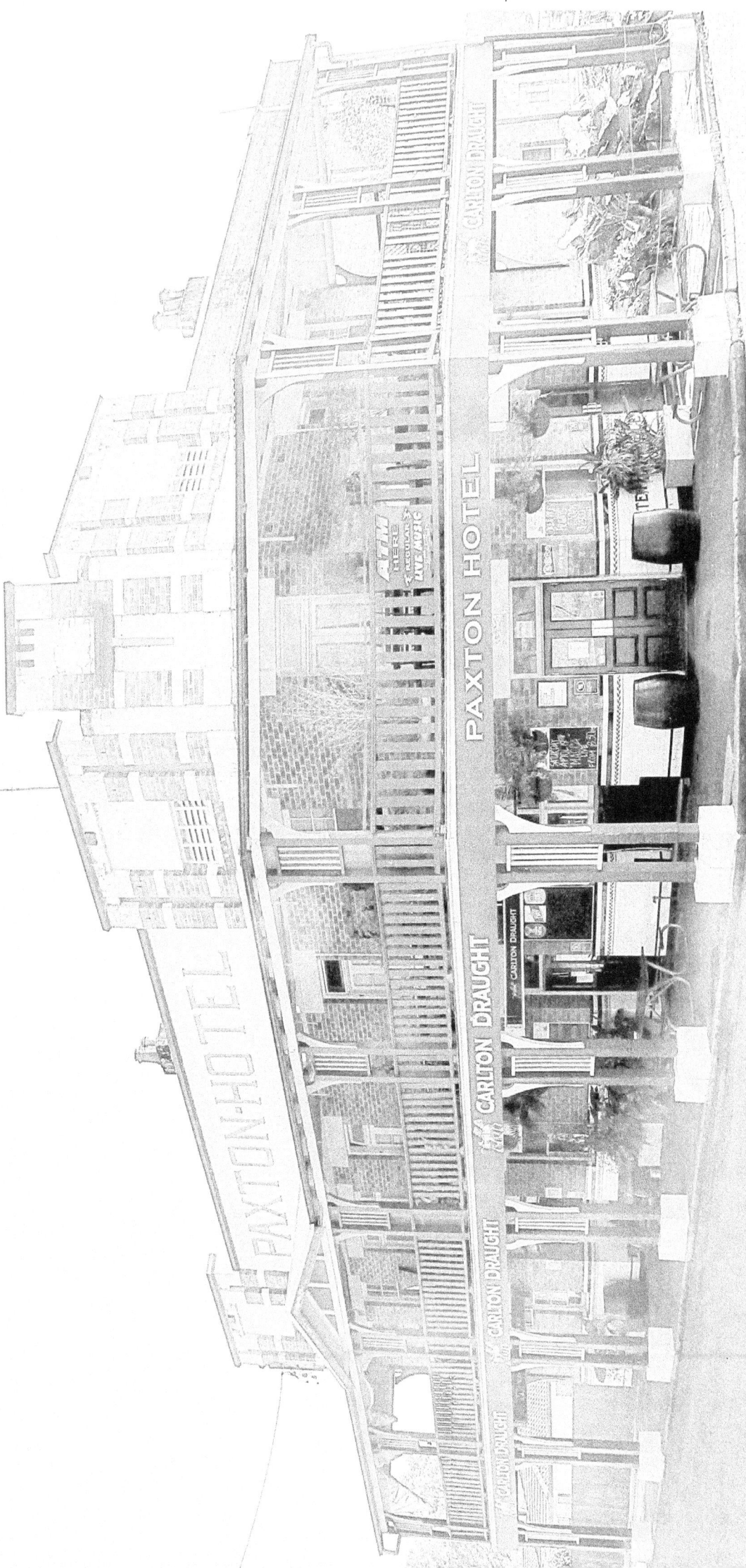

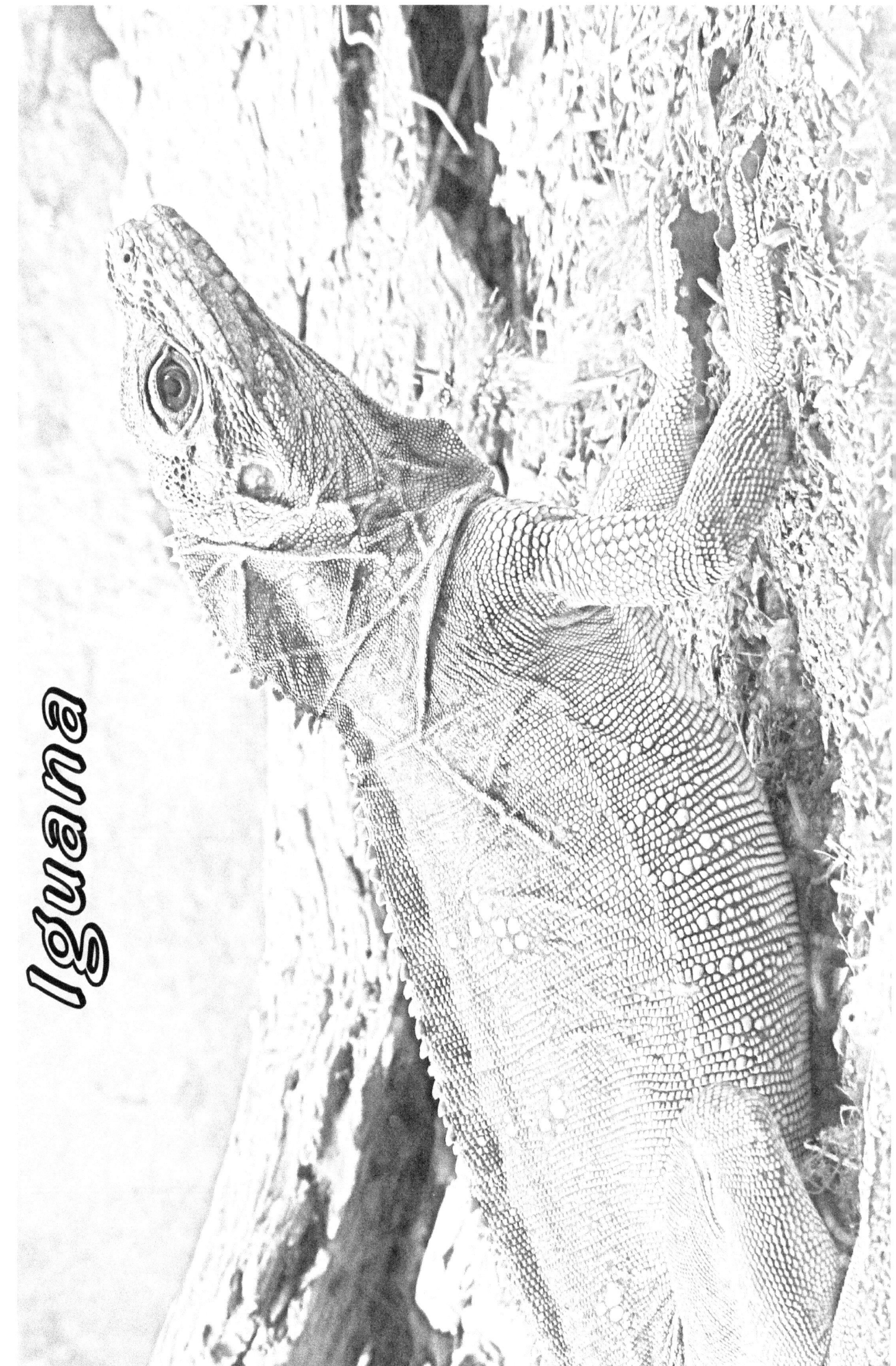

Iguana

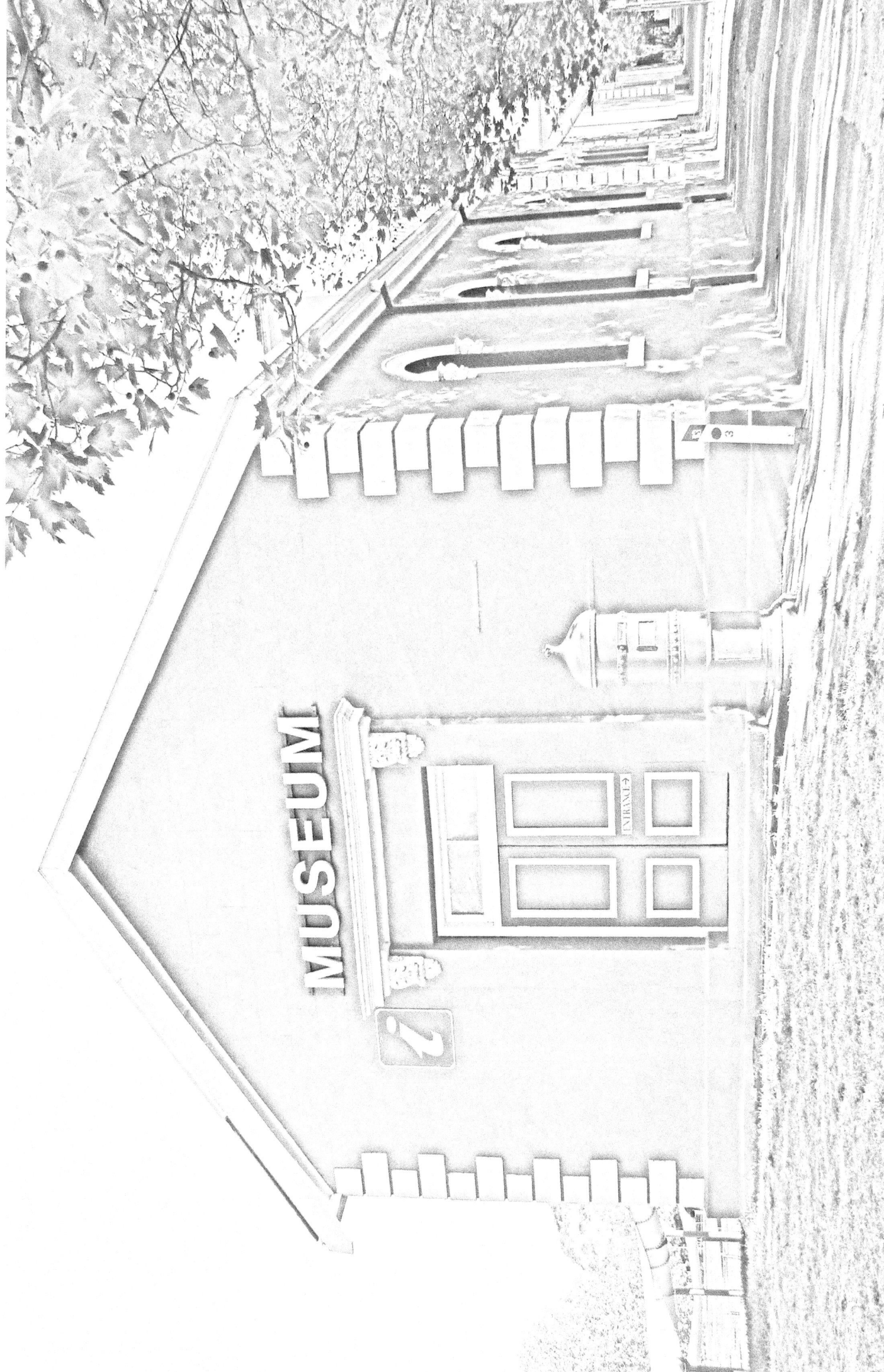

Parrots

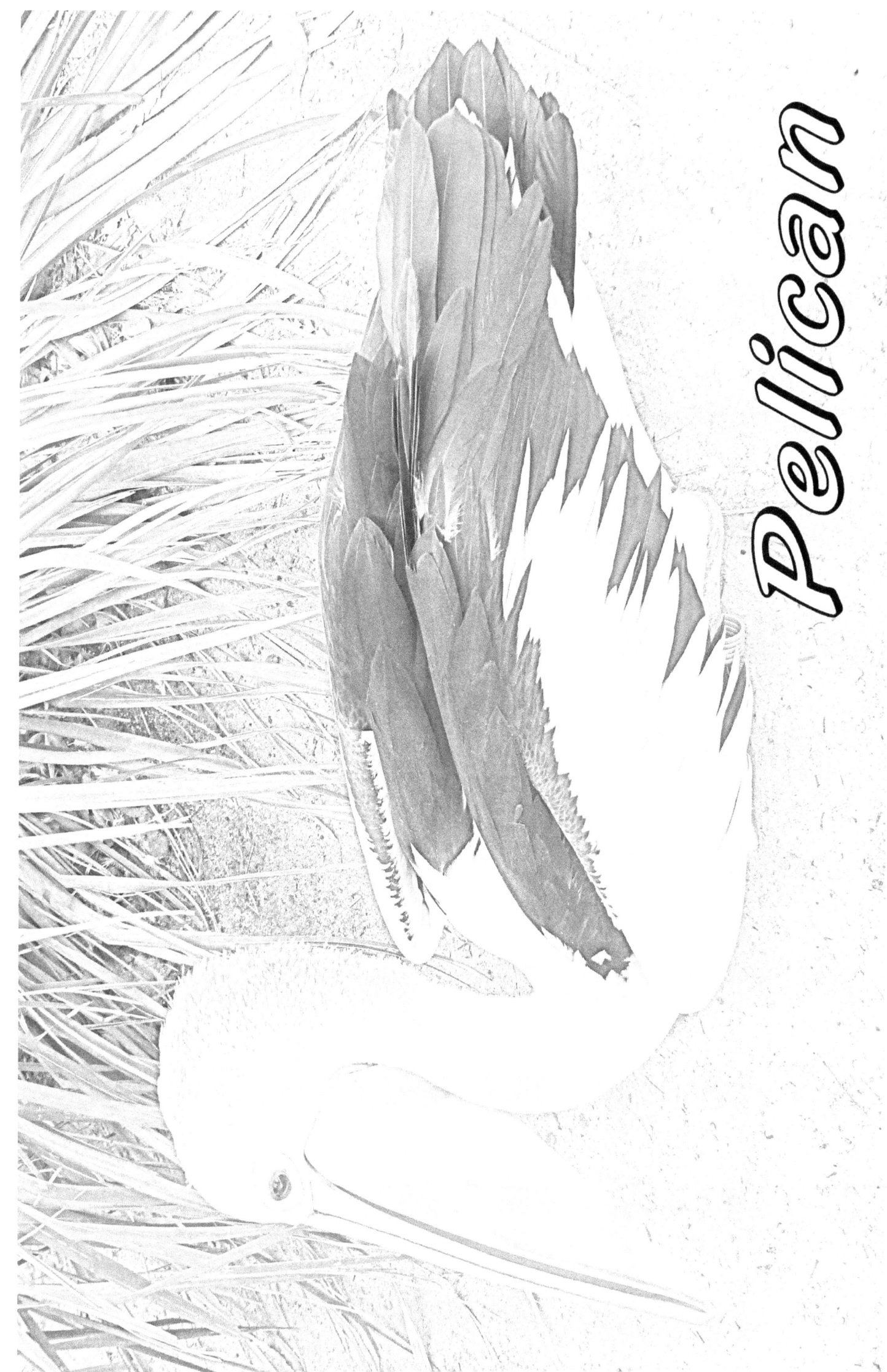

Pelican

Sailing

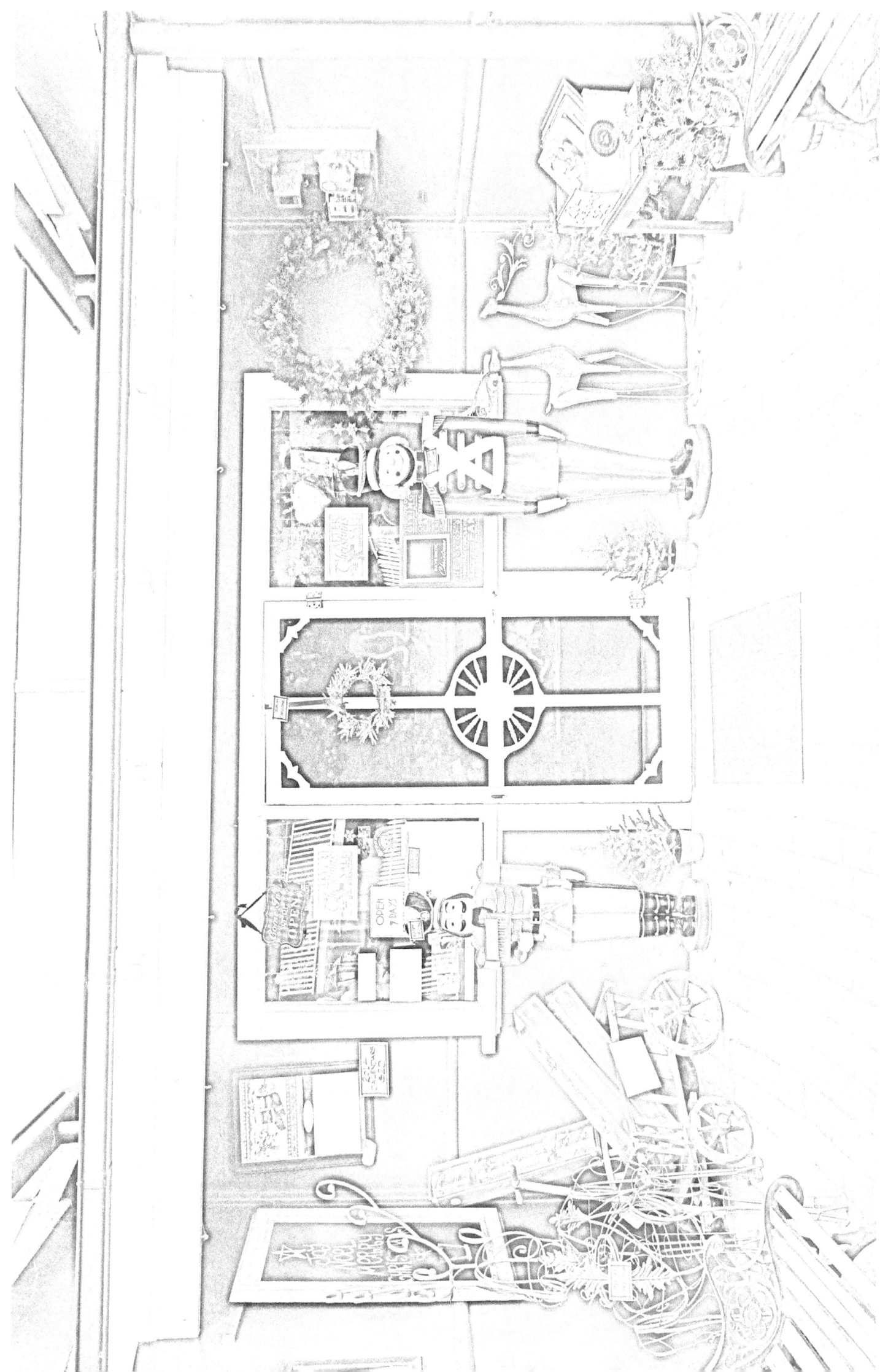

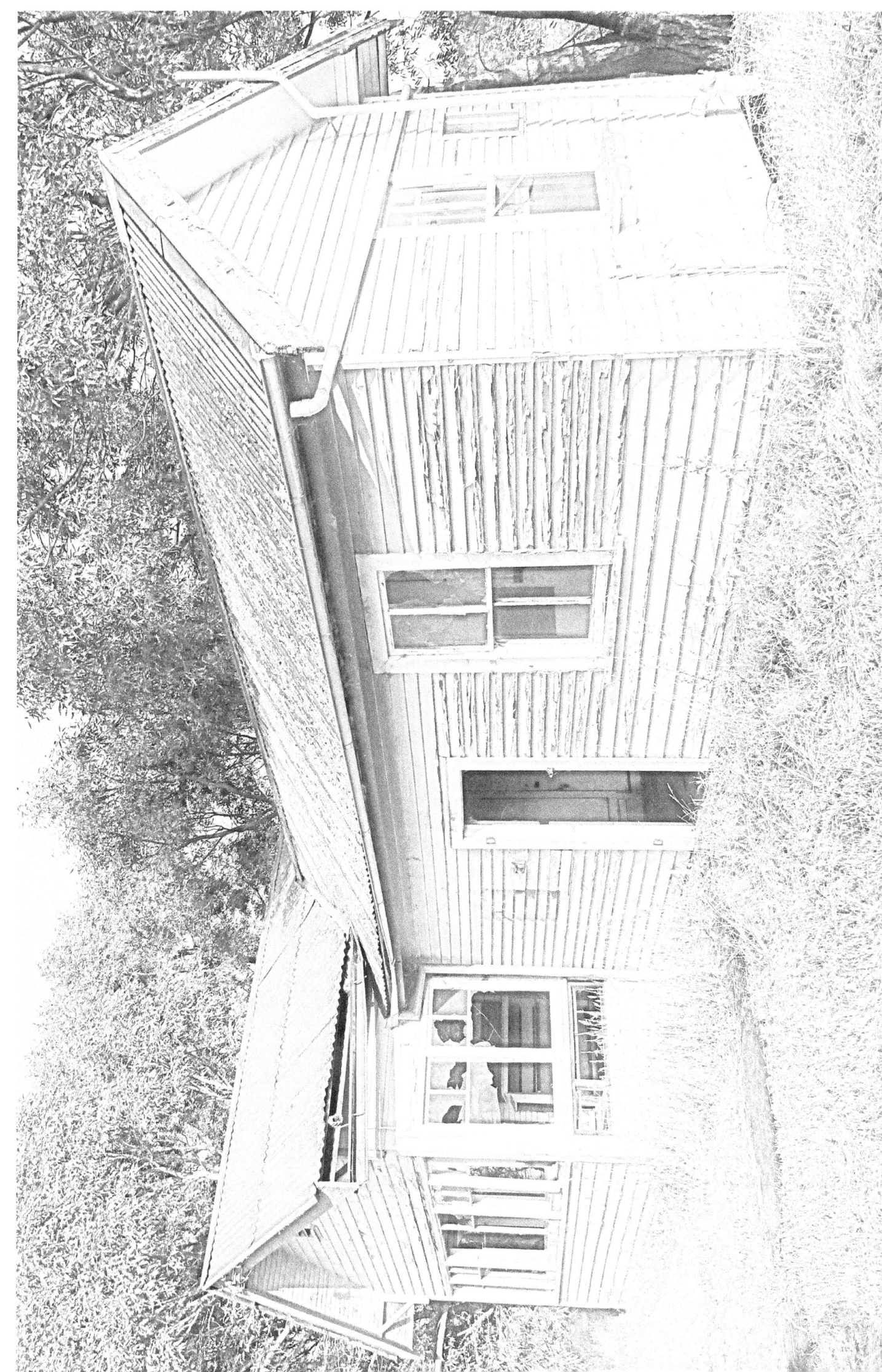

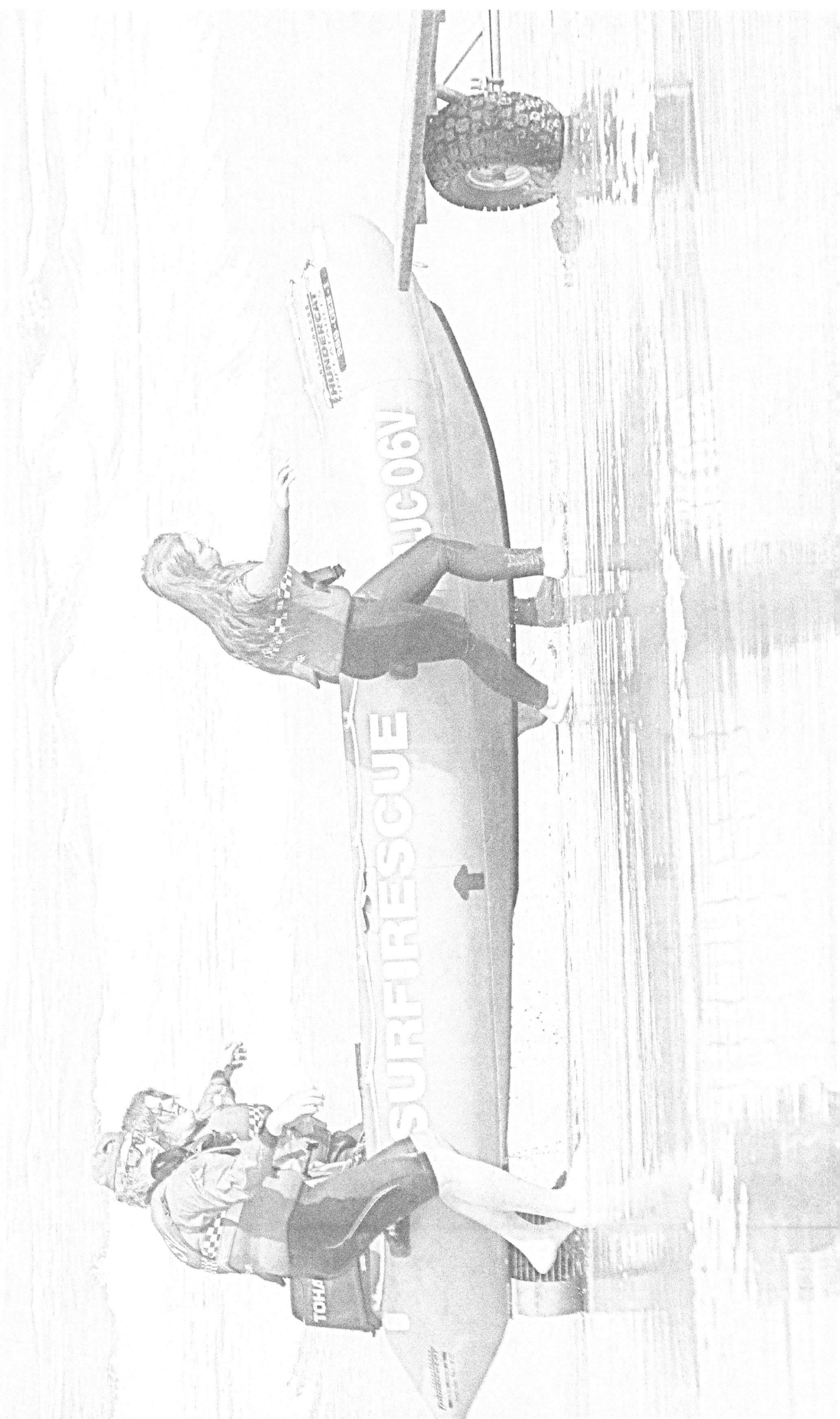

Tiger

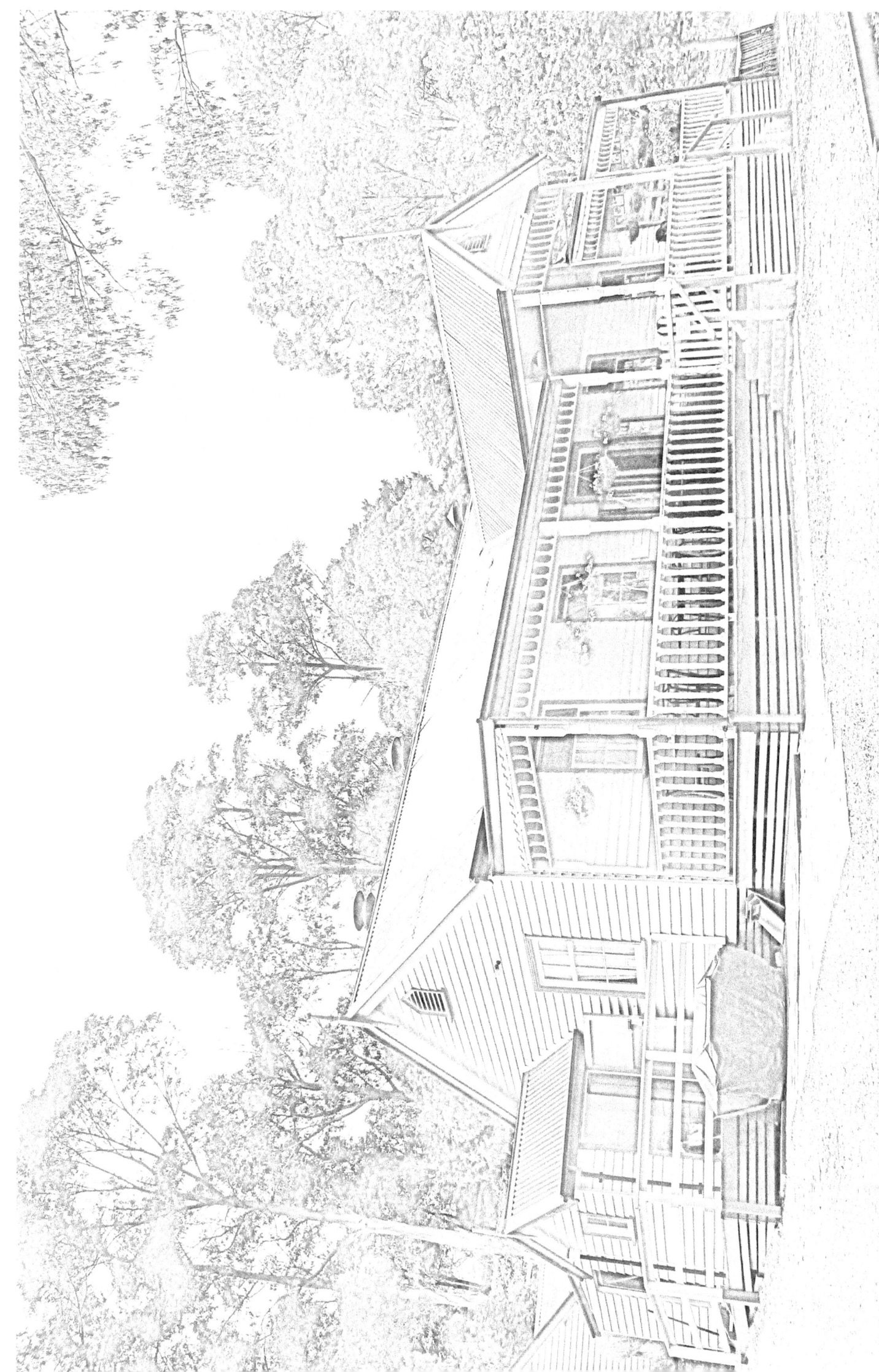

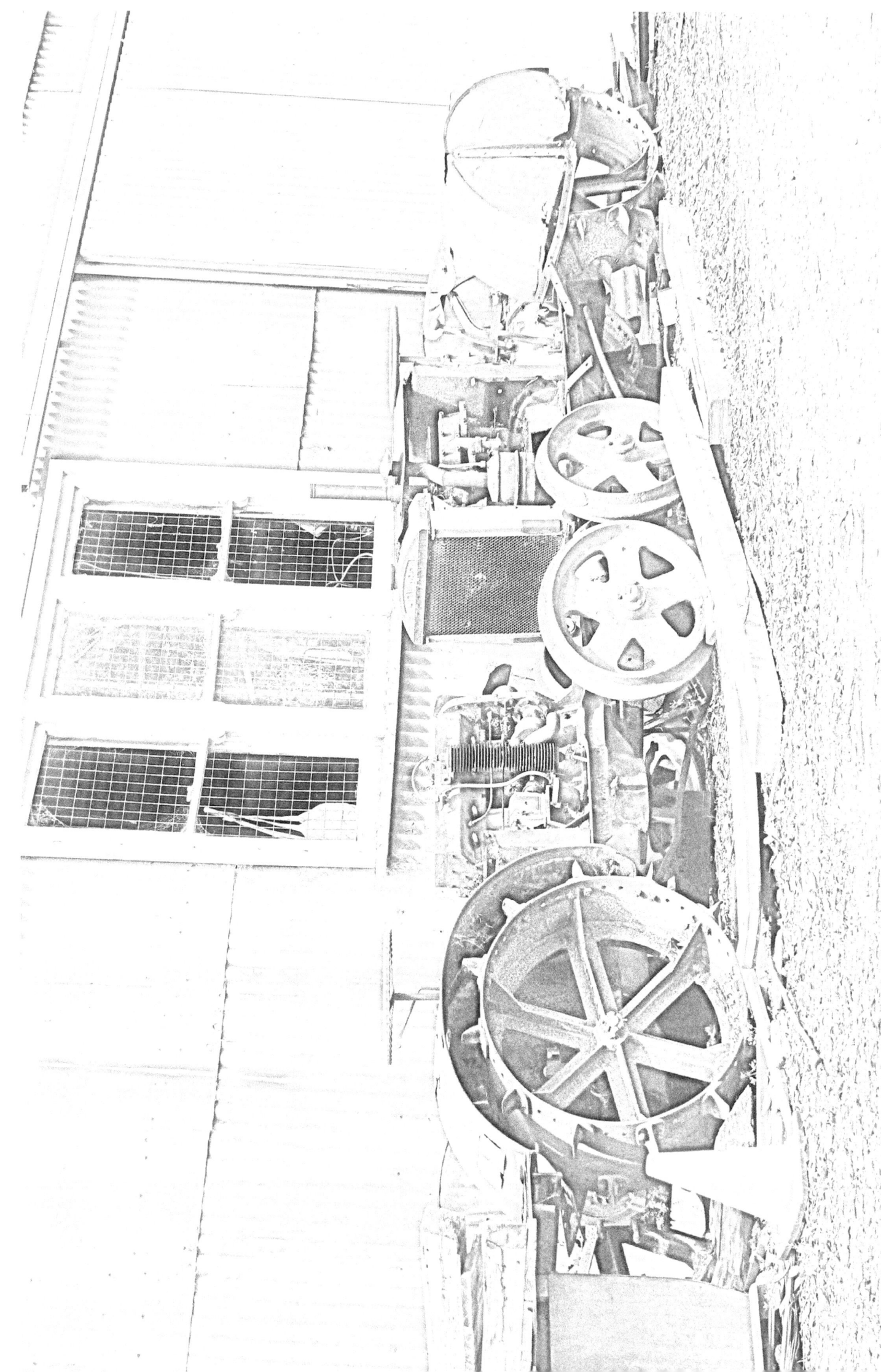

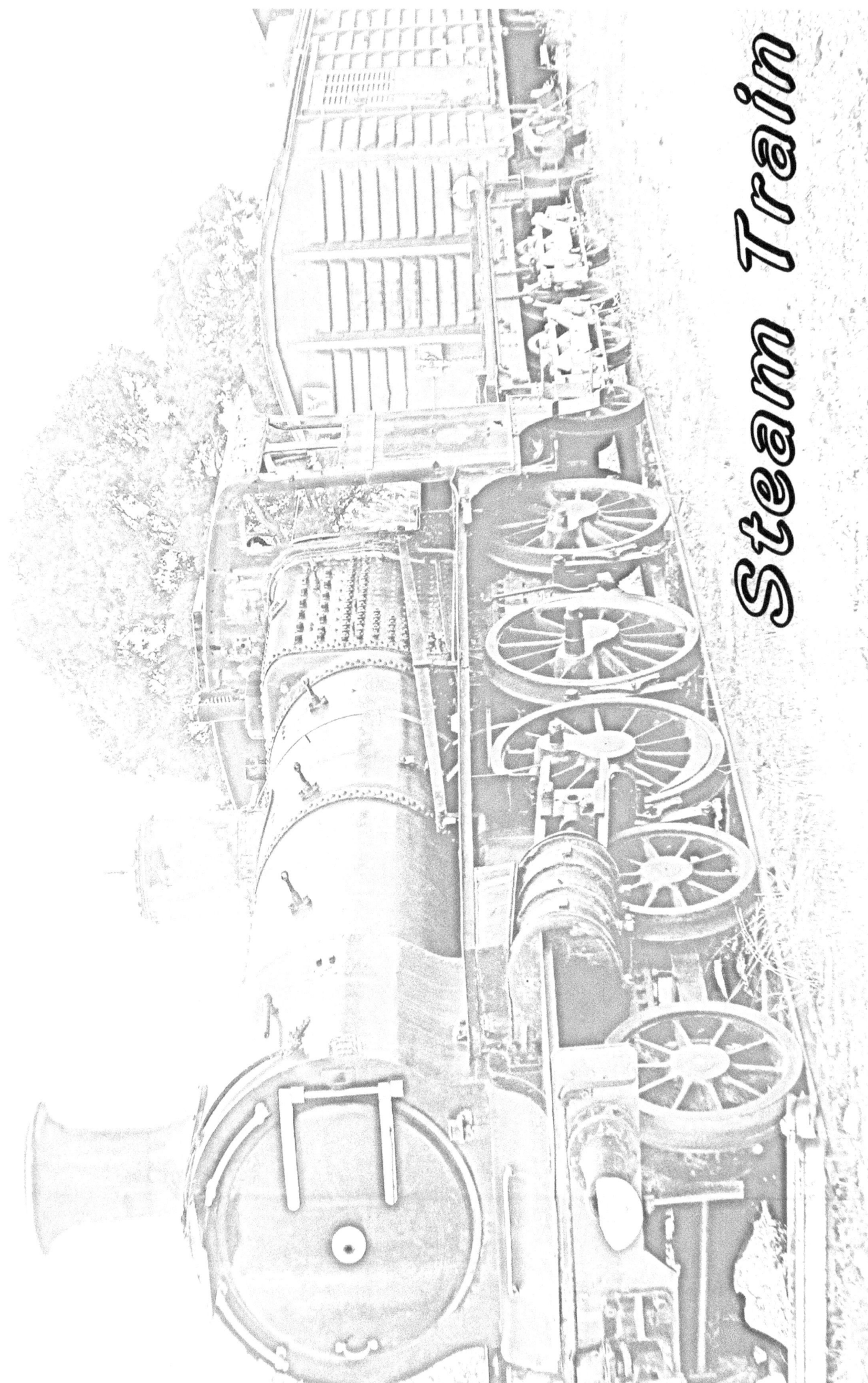

Steam Train

Tree Frog

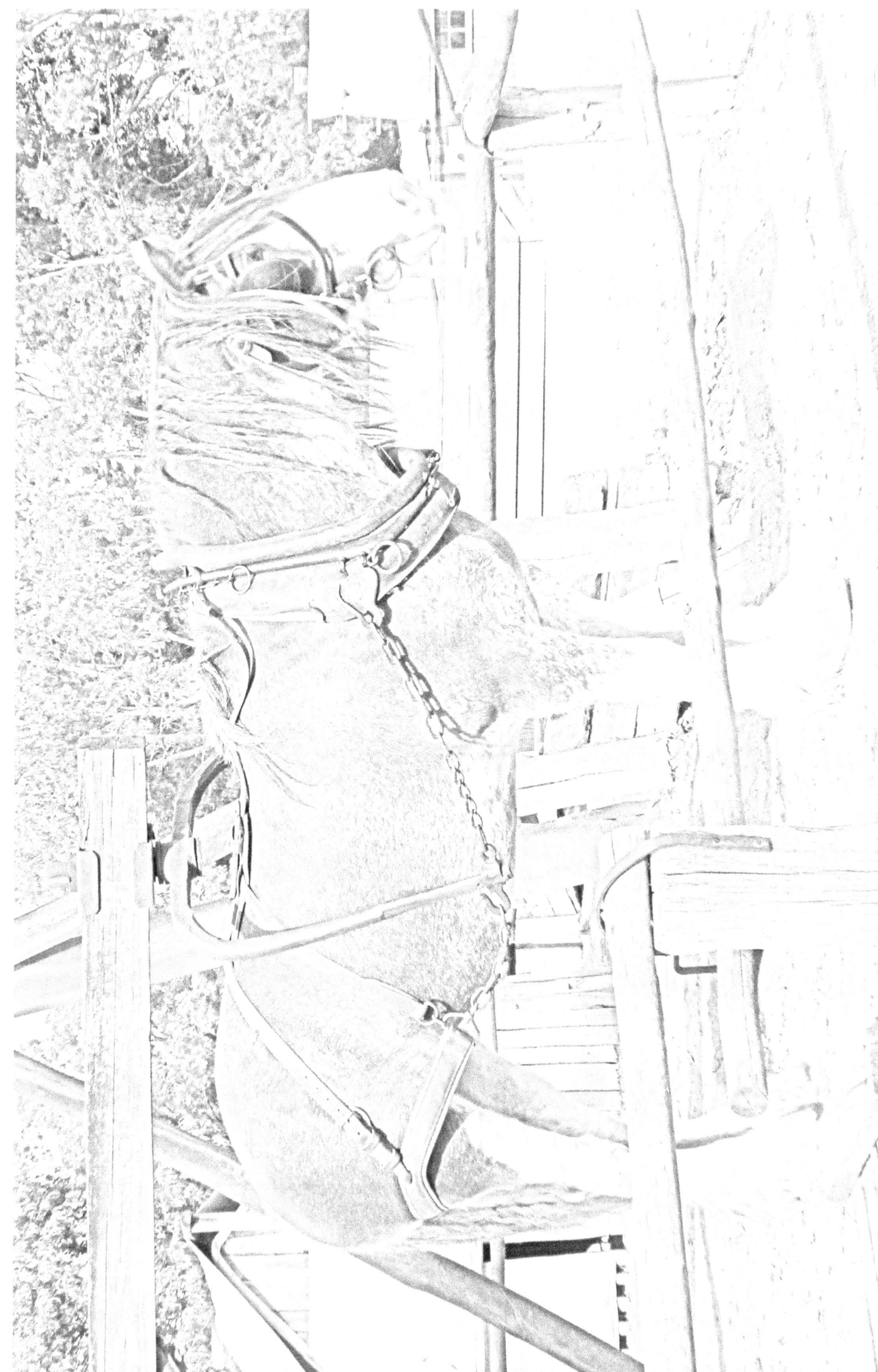

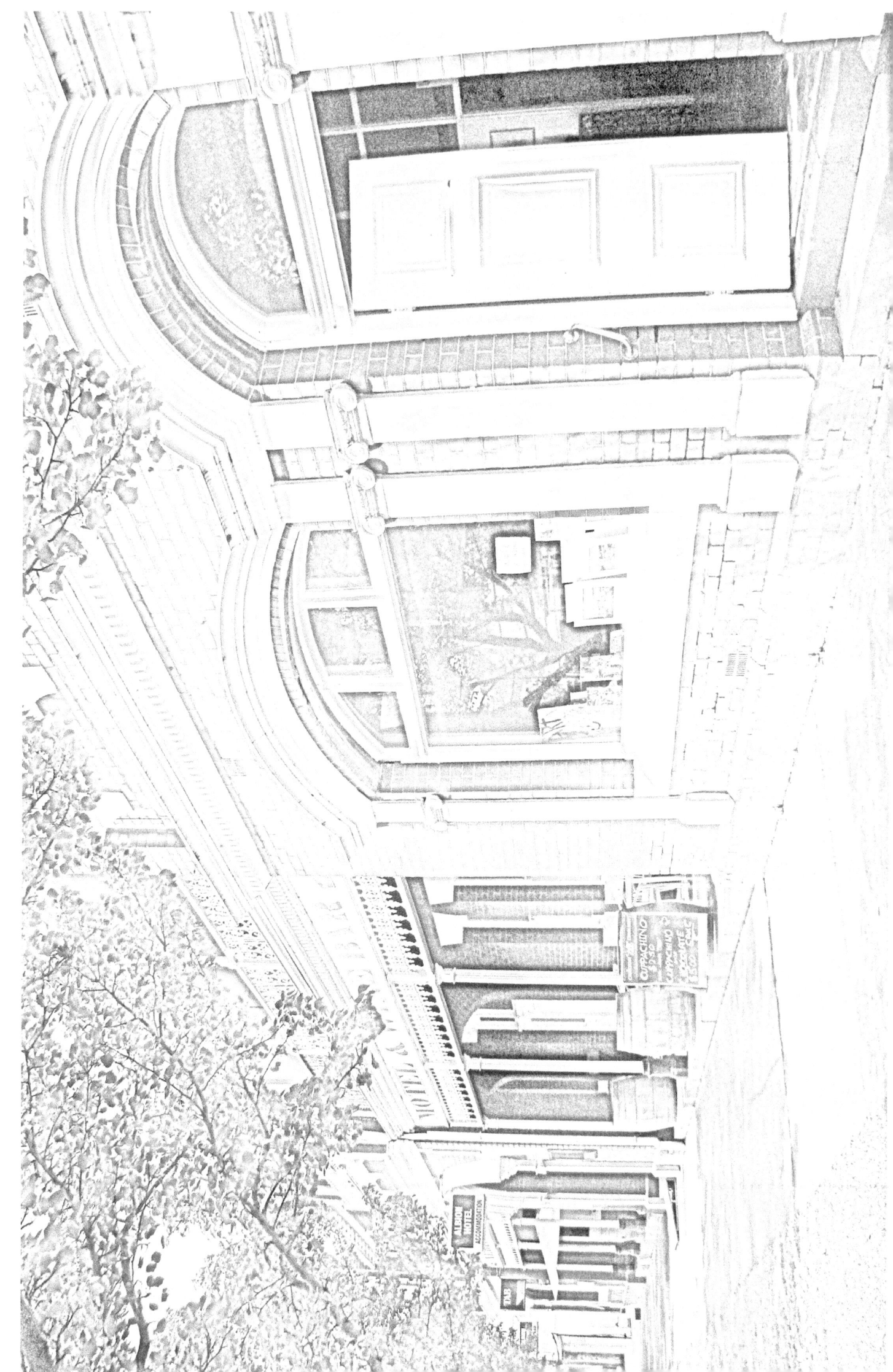

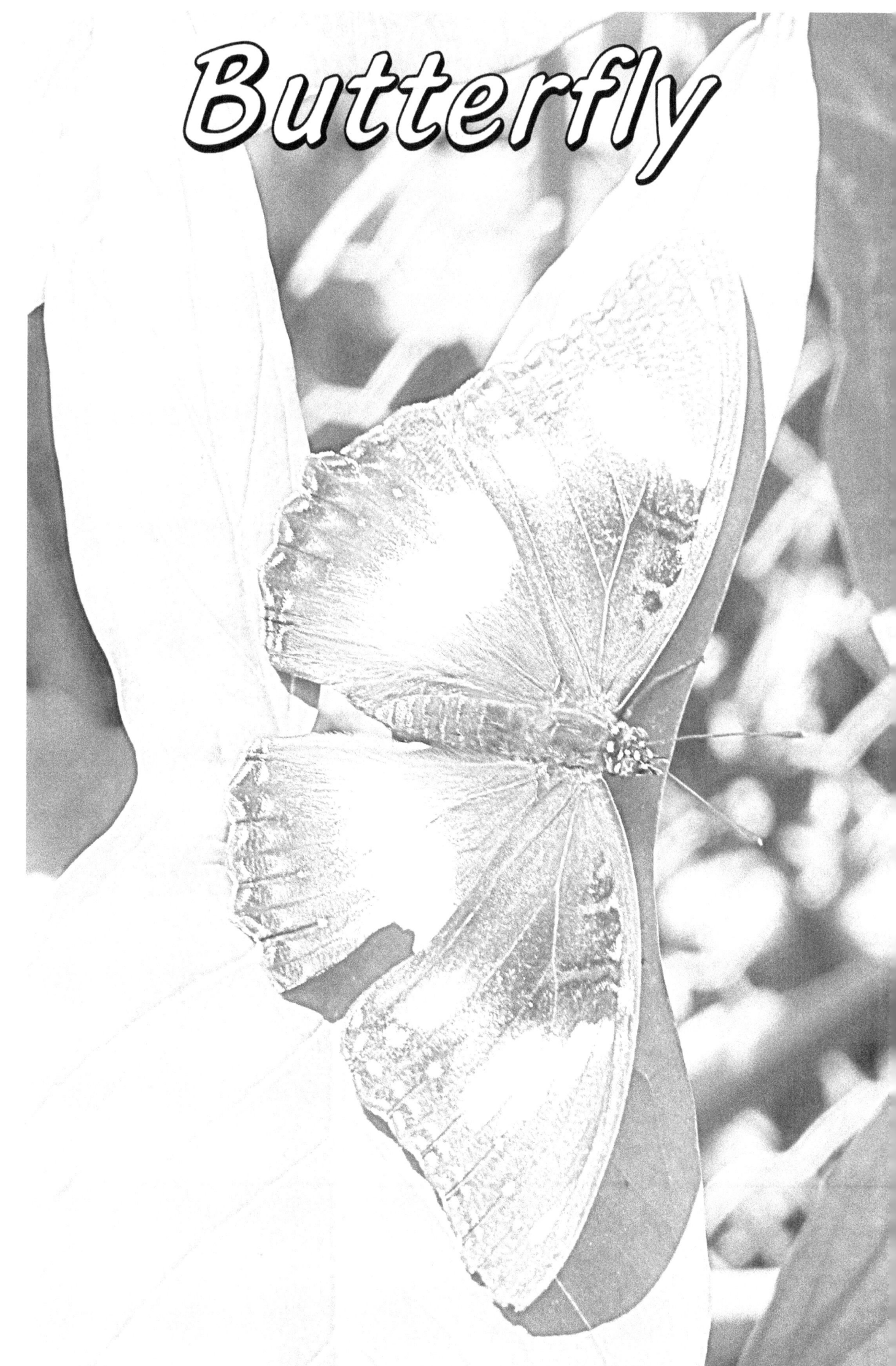

Butterfly

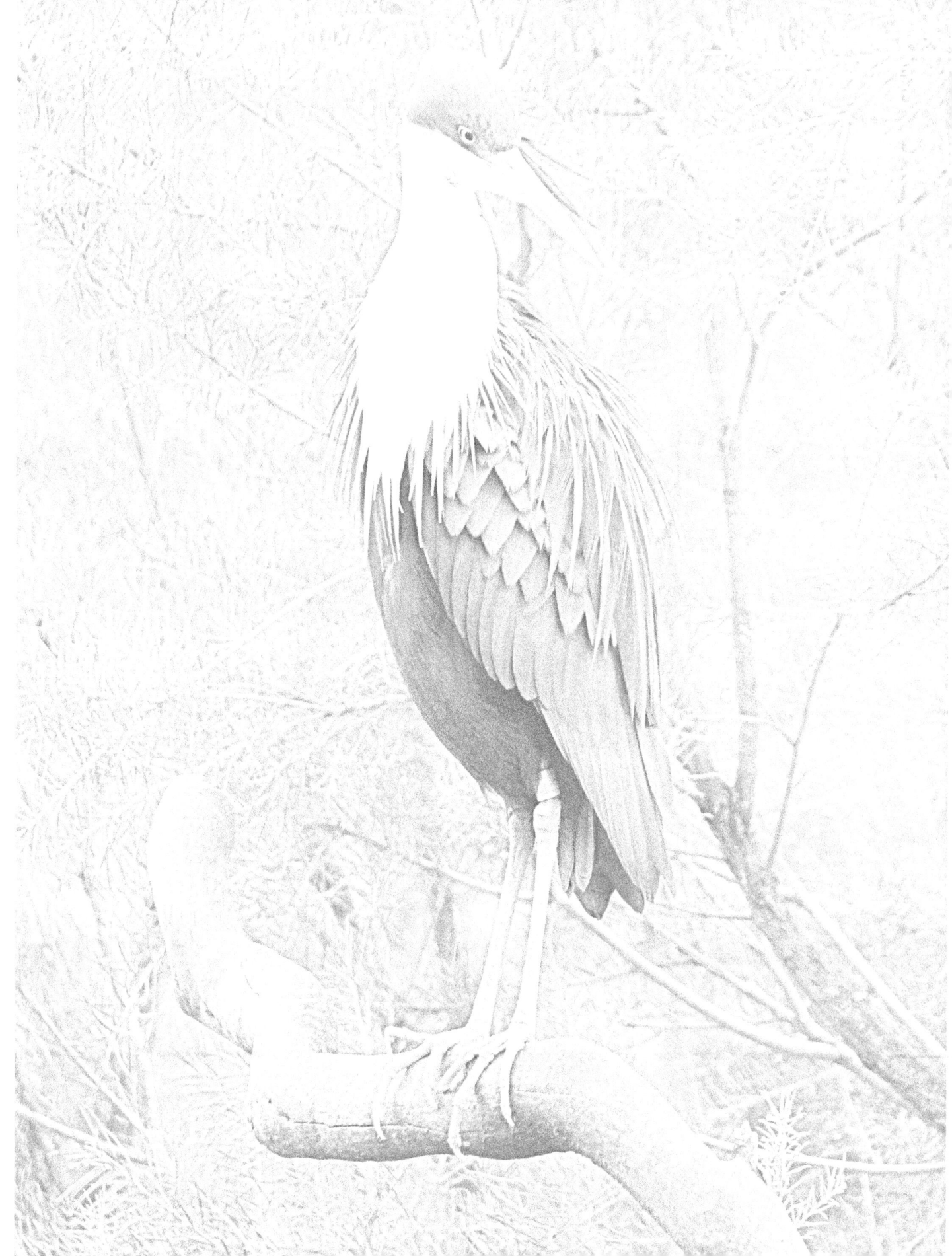

Crane

Fire Station

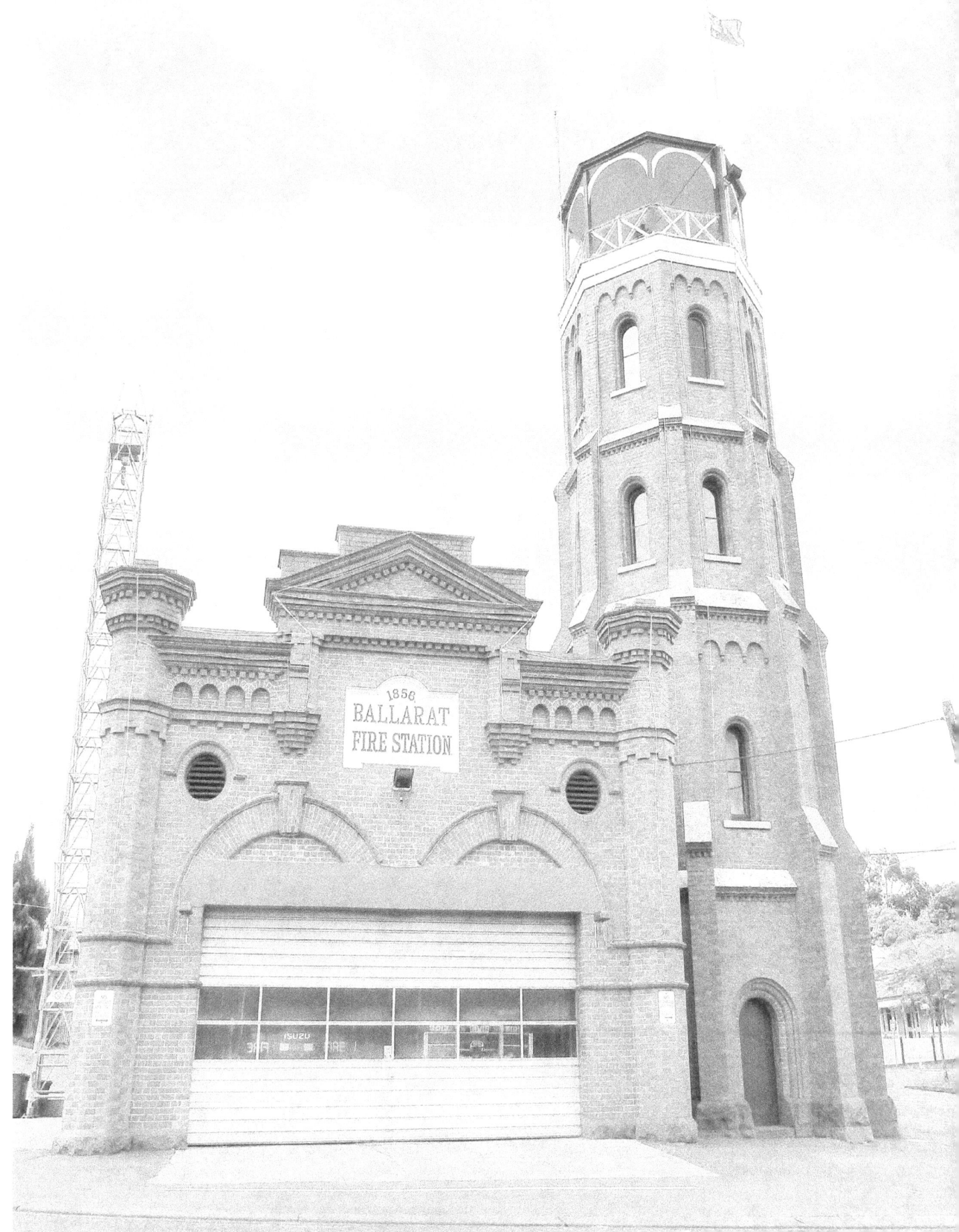

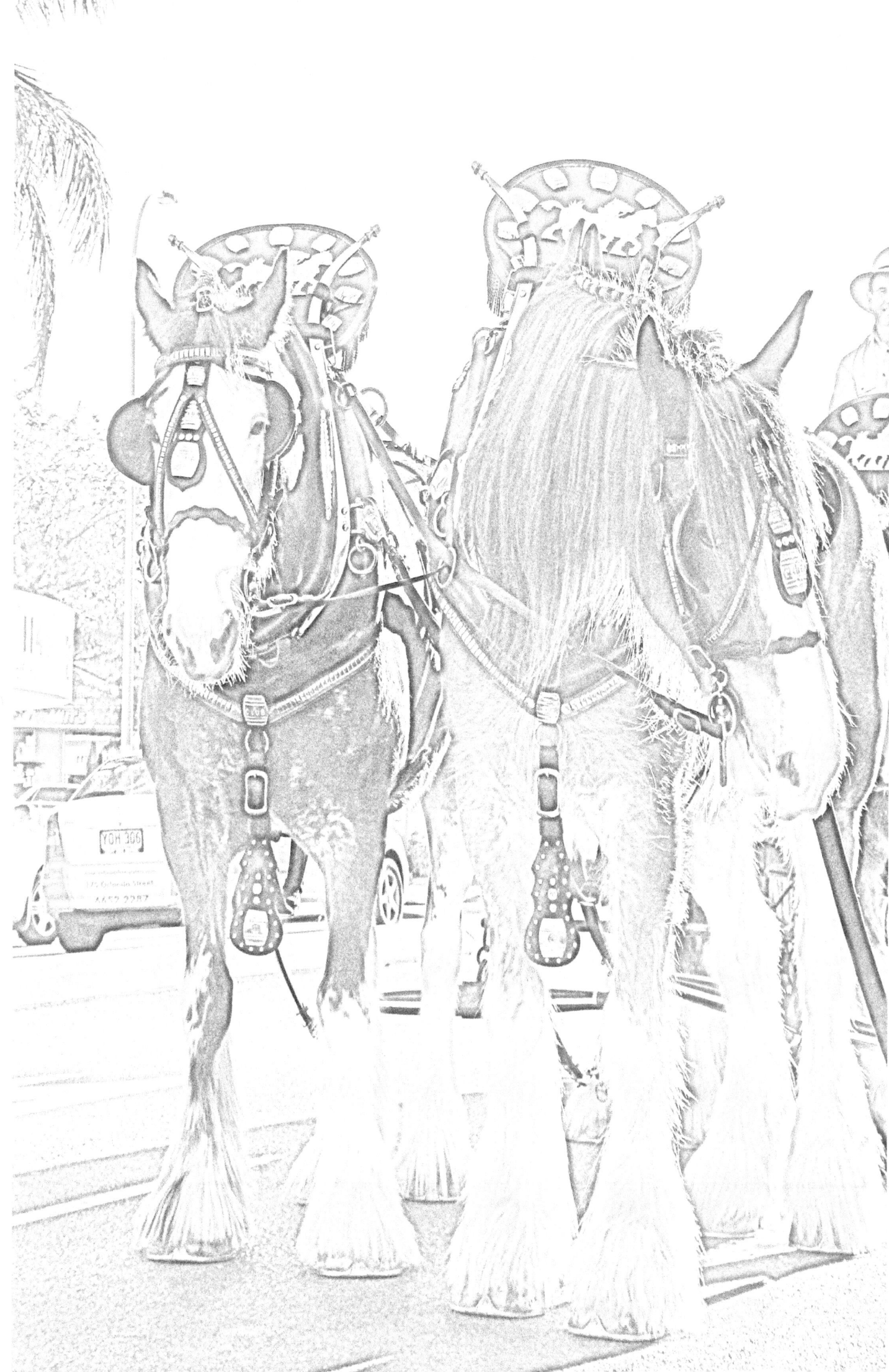

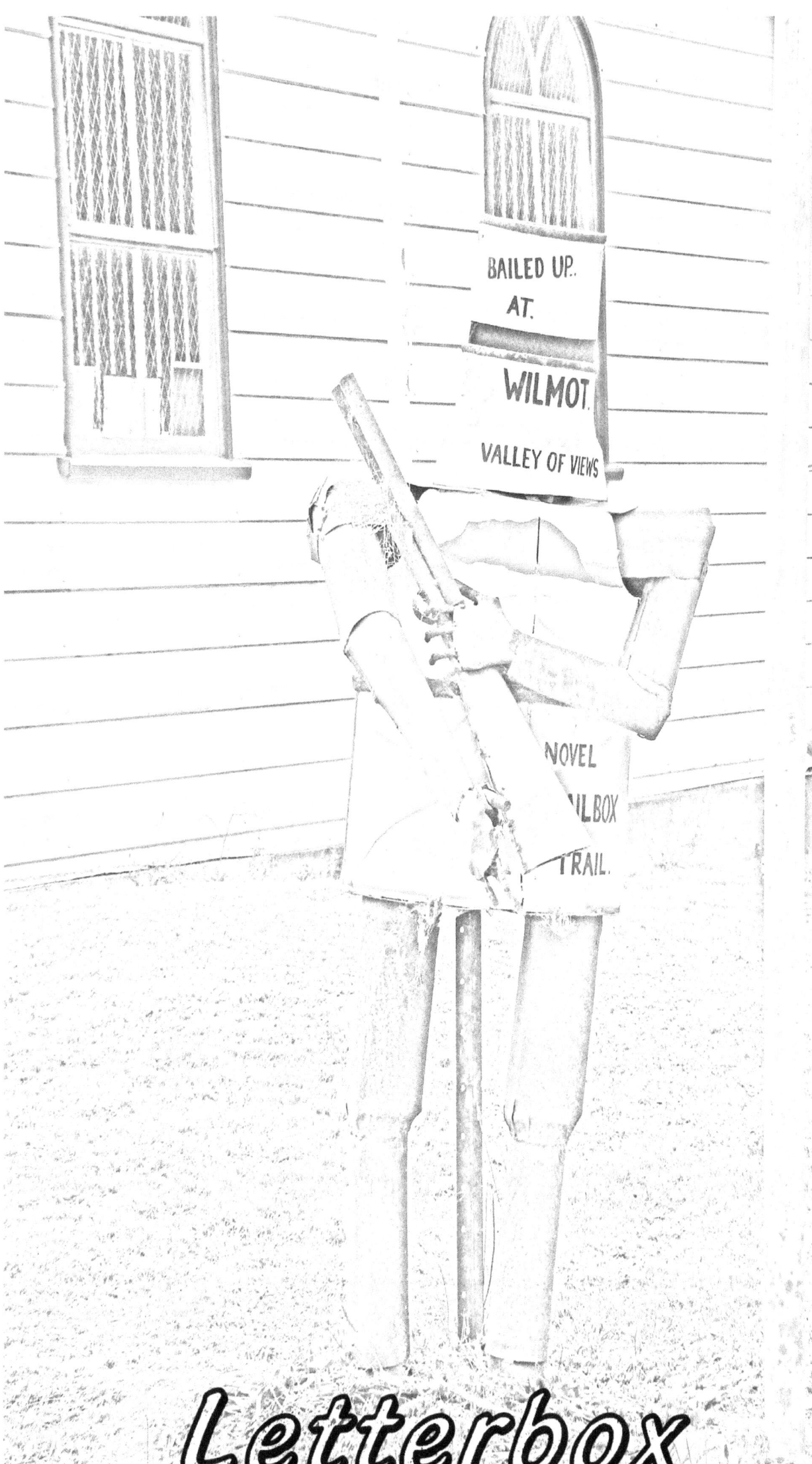

Letterbox

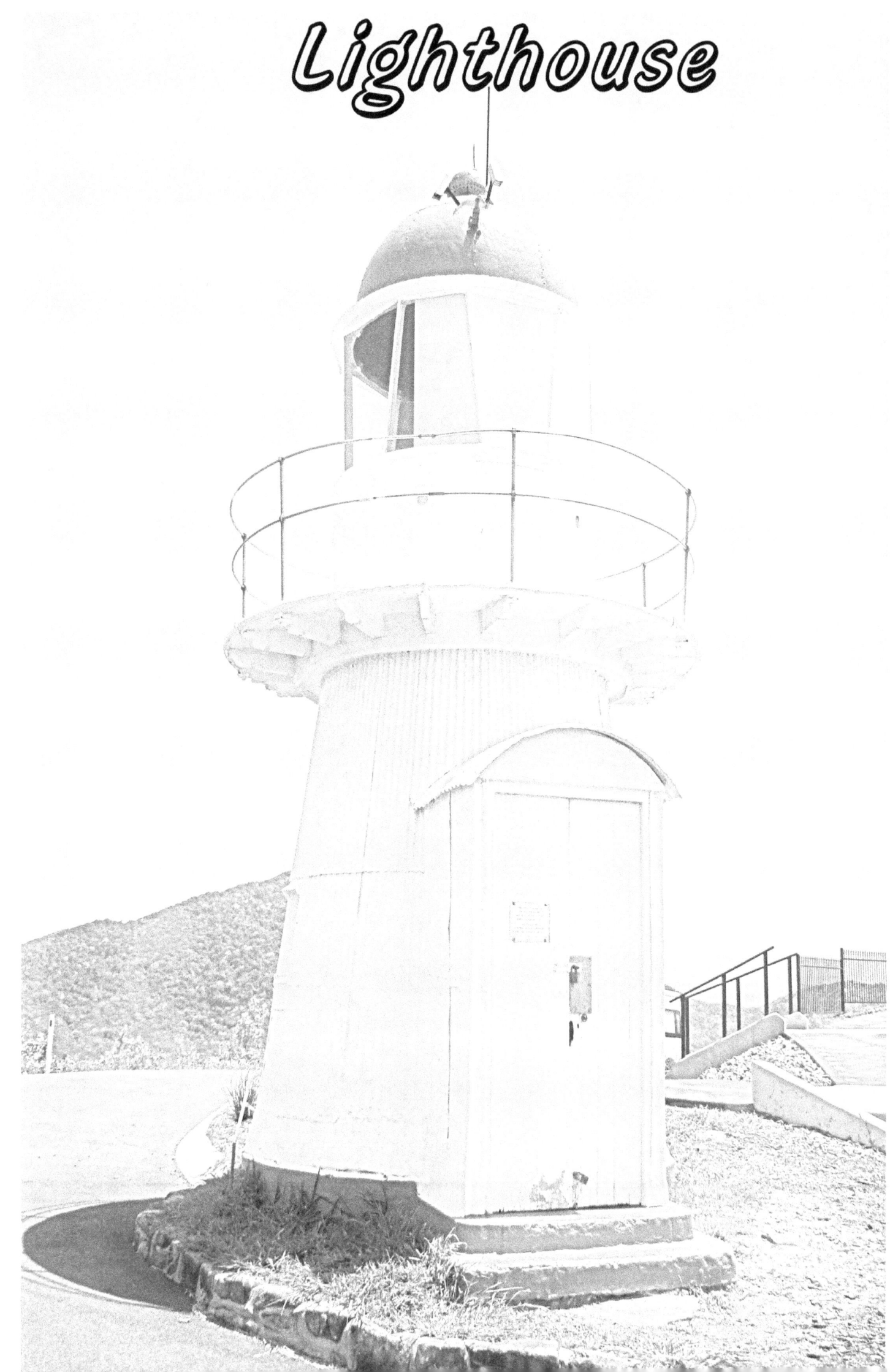

Lighthouse

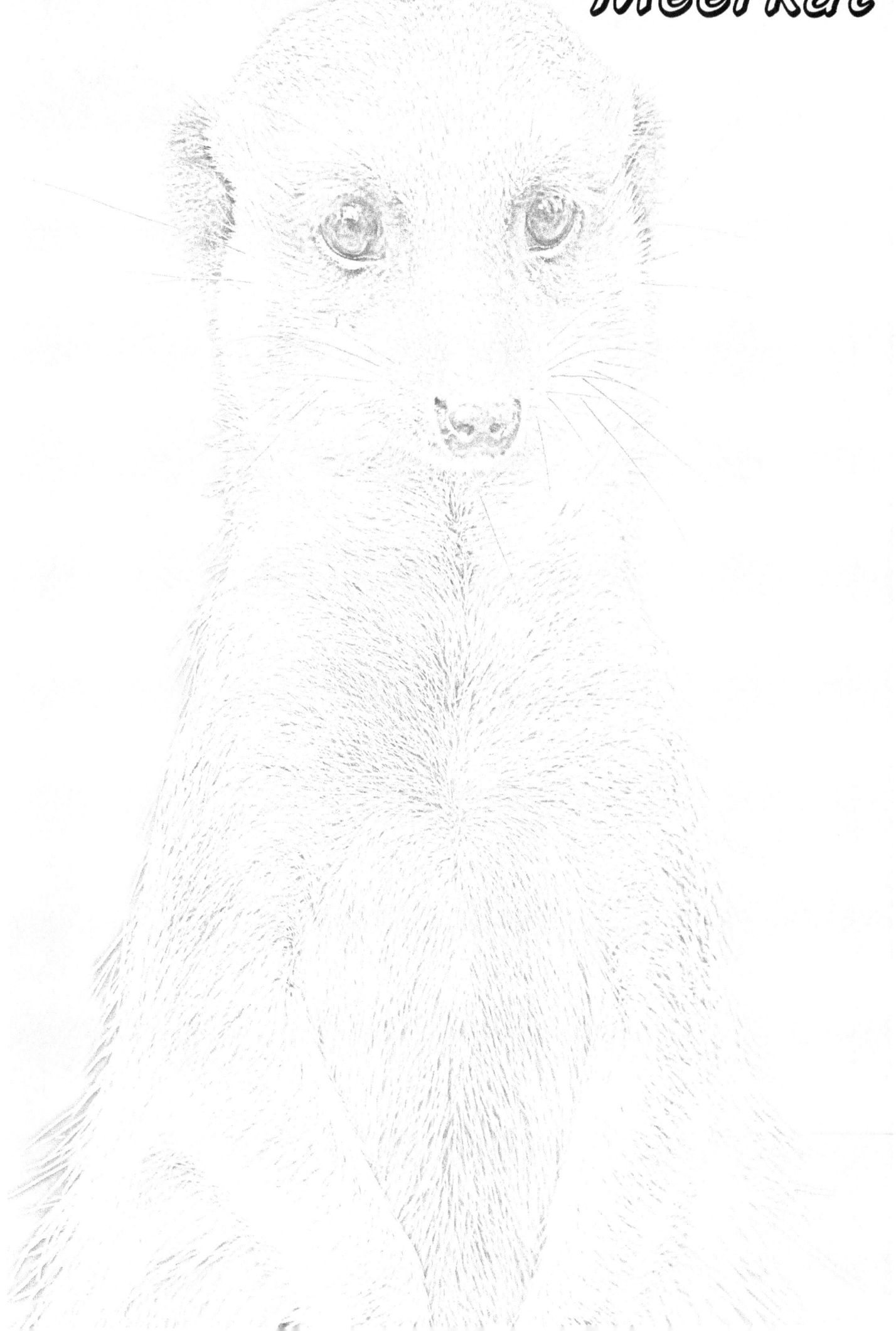

Meerkat

Monkey

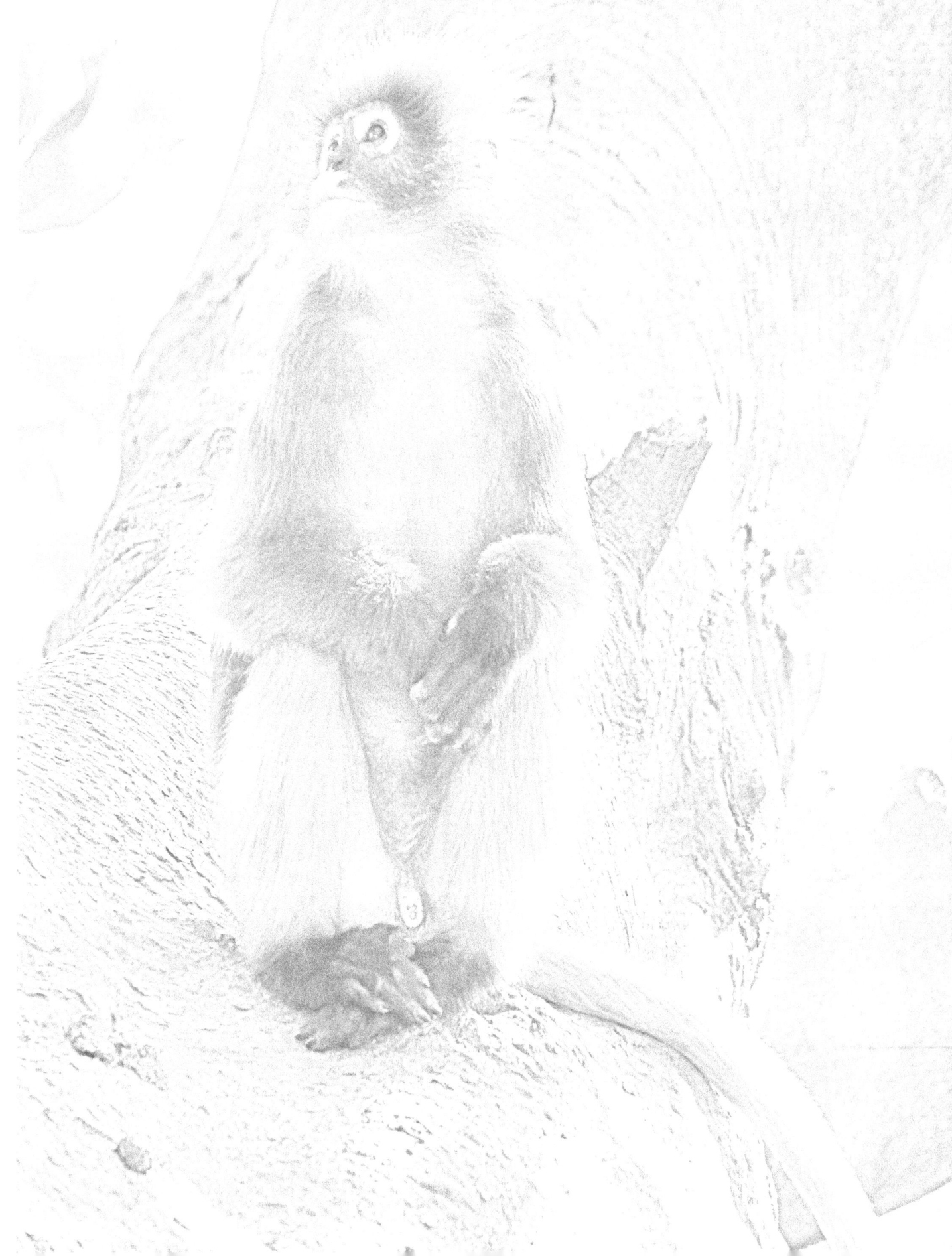

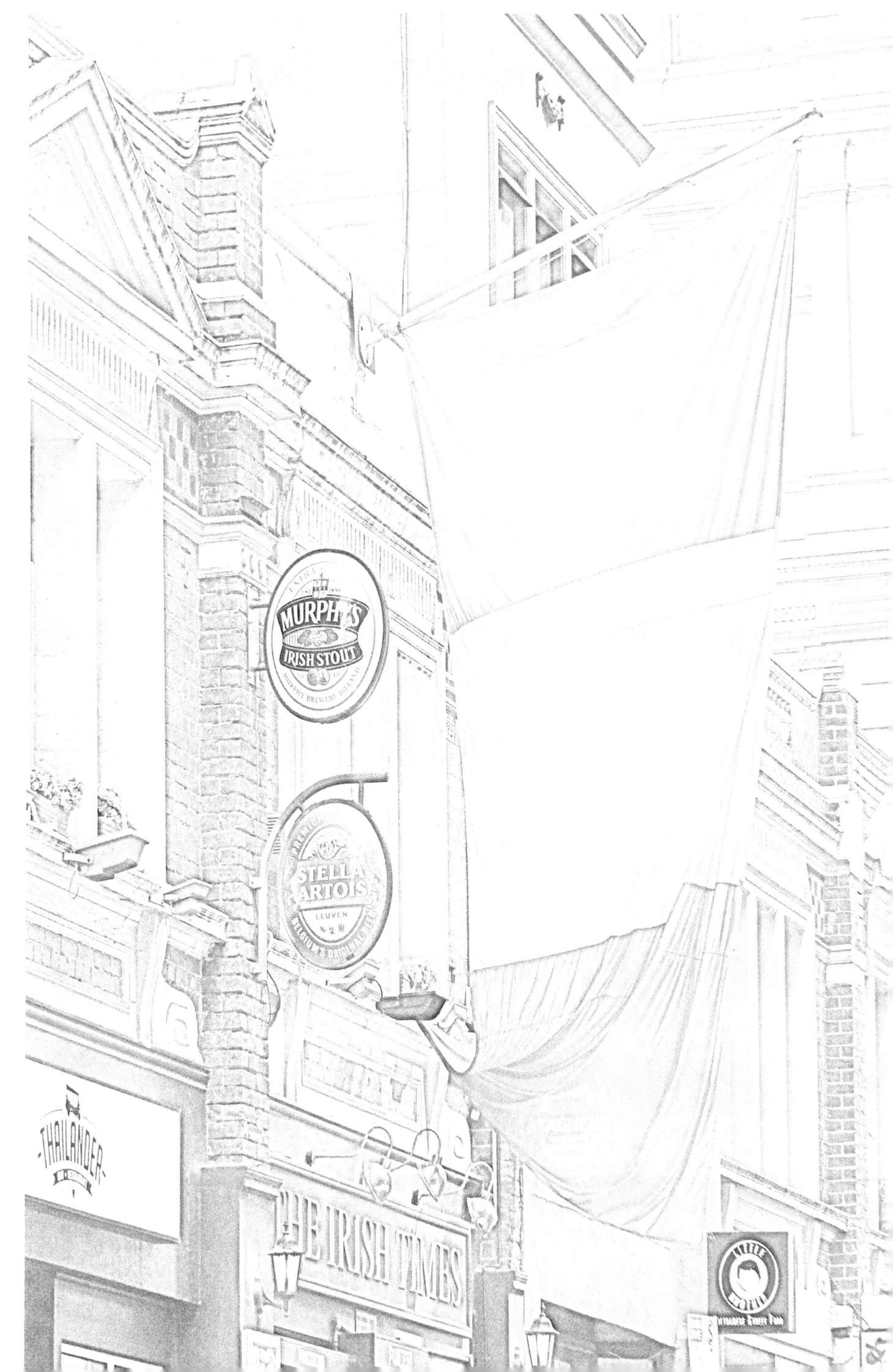

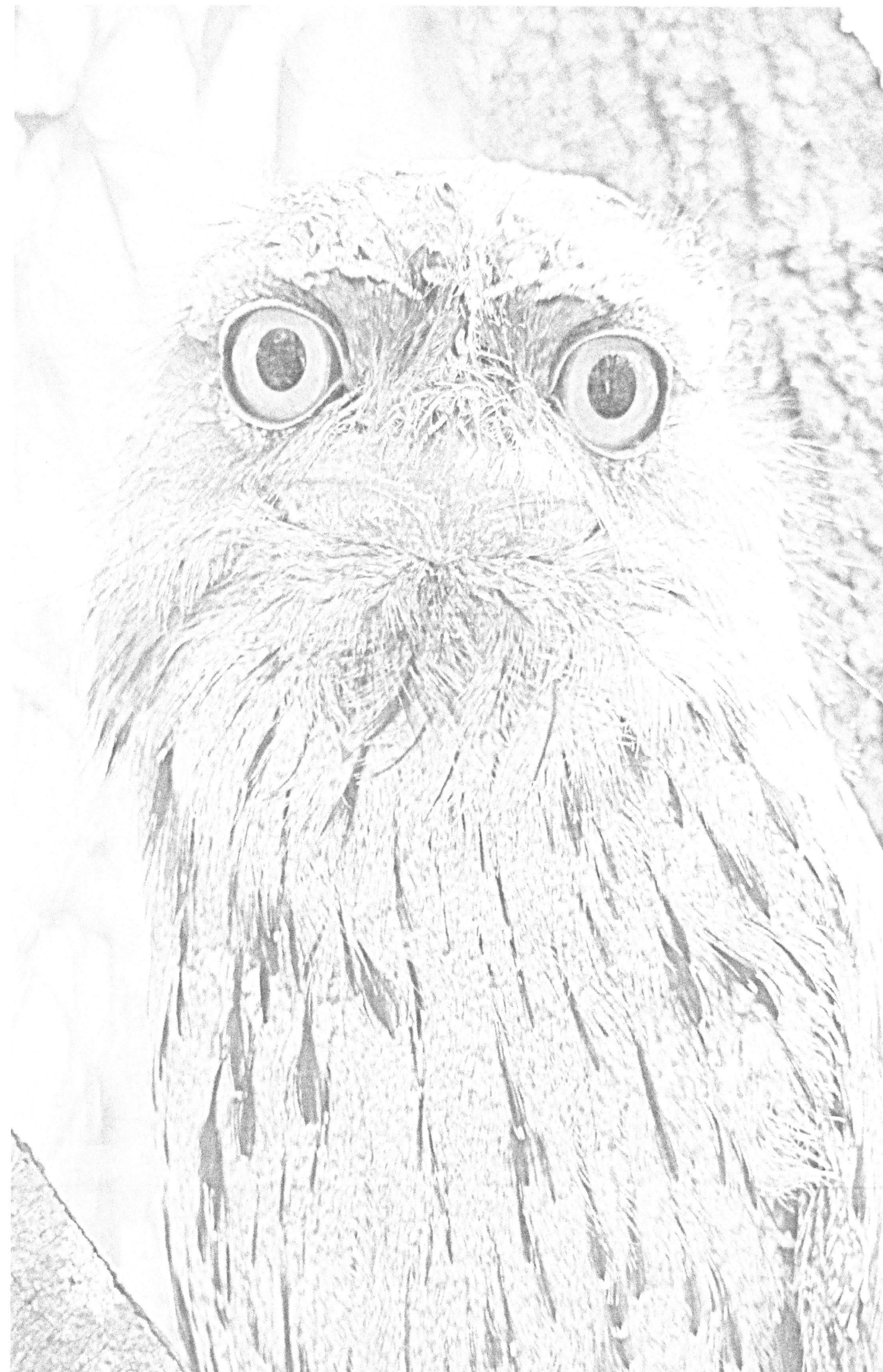